WHEN

STOPS CARING

❧

BETH MURRAY

Note for Librarians: A cataloguing record for this book is available from Library and
Archives Canada at www.collectionscanada.ca/amicus/index-e.html
ISBN 1-4120-5388-9

*Printed in Victoria, BC, Canada. Printed on paper with minimum 30% recycled fibre. Trafford's print shop
runs on "green energy" from solar, wind and other environmentally-friendly power sources.*

TRAFFORD

Offices in Canada, USA, Ireland and UK
This book was published *on-demand* in cooperation with Trafford Publishing. On-demand
publishing is a unique process and service of making a book available for retail sale
to the public taking advantage of on-demand manufacturing and Internet marketing.
On-demand publishing includes promotions, retail sales, manufacturing, order fulfilment,
accounting and collecting royalties on behalf of the author.

Book sales for North America and international:
Trafford Publishing, 6E–2333 Government St.,
Victoria, BC v8t 4p4 CANADA
phone 250 383 6864 (toll-free 1 888 232 4444)
fax 250 383 6804; email to orders@trafford.com
Book sales in Europe:
Trafford Publishing (uk) Ltd., Enterprise House, Wistaston Road Business Centre,
Wistaston Road, Crewe, Cheshire cw2 7rp UNITED KINGDOM
phone 01270 251 396 (local rate 0845 230 9601)
facsimile 01270 254 983; orders.uk@trafford.com
Order online at:
trafford.com/05-0283

10 9 8 7 6 5

This book is dedicated to my Mum and Dad.
Thank you for teaching me about what it means to care—
for bringing me up in the church,
and establishing me in my faith.

CONTENTS

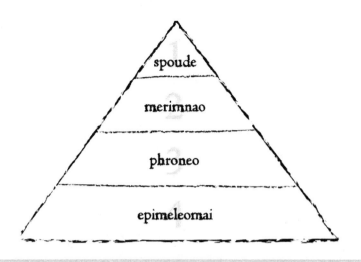

My Care Experience

I remember sitting in my pastor's office approximately 10 years ago. I was a single parent with two boys, going through the throes of divorce (which incidentally should be called the "throws" of divorce!) and attending college full-time. I was on my way to fulfilling God's call on my life, to become a Christian counsellor and be involved in full-time ministry. However, at this point in time, slumped dejectedly in the pastor's office, my honorable call seemed far beyond reach! I was living on a shoe-string financially, eking my existence out of a student loan and some grant money.

My boys were young, ages 3 and 5, and I was doing my classes at night, so I could be with them during the day. I was emotionally, mentally, physically and financially beyond exhaustion. I was living in the city's subsidized housing, the "projects" as some people labeled them! The boys and I moved away from family and friends so I could attend college, and even though we were less than an hour from home, it felt like the other side of the Nile! I was lonely and desperately in need of support and care. Hence my arrival at the pastor's office.

The stresses of life, single parenting, a depleted immune system, and trying to do school work, were taking their toll! It's not like I was a total waste of skin– I had skills and talents. In fact, I was really quite resilient due to the powerful grace and faithfulness of Christ. Yet that day, I felt a knot wad up in the pit of my stomach. As we discussed my situation, the pastor drew five concentric circles. He was sharing the vision of the church with me. It was a fairly young church plant, with close to 150 people attending. The circles outlined their strategy for corporate worship and drama, discipleship, evangelism and other exciting and trendy hopes. When he was finished the drawing, he drew a small loop at the end of one of the circles. The meagerly dwarfed circle, he informed me, represented people like me. "Like me?" I questioned. "Yes," he replied, "needy people."

"Needy?" I ran the word over and over in my mind, stunned, trying to comprehend what had just been said. He went on, "It's just that…well…we really aren't equipped to deal with someone like you. Someone, well…who has so many needs." He smiled, as if the artistic drawing would somehow take away the sting of what I had just heard! He nodded and tried to make eye contact with me, hoping to evoke my agreement. All I had asked for was the opportunity to join a small group! To do that, I needed someone to pay for my babysitting (or have the group chip in on a babysitter, or allow children to come), or to have the group at my house, so I didn't have to get a babysitter. In a church of 150 people that placed me into the

meagerly dwarfed circle of the "needy?!" Sigh.

God used that experience to do an interesting work in my heart. As I poured my hurt out to my counsellor the following week, she asked me what was wrong with being needy. I felt my blood pressure begin to ascend. "I'm not needy!" I retorted.

"Okay, but what is so wrong with being needy?"

I told her how I hated the sound of the word, the utter weakness that it conjured up. Wrong answer! My homework assignment: to look up every incidence of the word "needy" as it appeared in scripture. What a humbling experience! I discovered numerous references to the needy, and they were always in a place of favour with God. It's as though God has a special place in His heart for the needy.

The Hebrew word for needy is *ebyown* (eb-yone), "in the sense of want (especially in feeling)," which comes from the word *abah* (aw-baw) which means "to breathe after; consent, rest content, will, be willing."[1] Wow! Maybe needy wasn't so bad after all! It was just an admittance of my own want and unfulfilled desires, taking me to a place of facing my own weakness and need. Through my own admission of desperate need for my God, He released a newness of His Spirit in me, and I discovered what being needy was really all about. I started "to breathe after" God like I never had in all my years of being a believer. I became more and more content with my need and weakness, even writing a song based on II Cor. 12:9, "my strength is made perfect in weakness." Perhaps strength can only be made perfect in weakness.

Unfortunately, a second scenario that all too often occurs in the church is not lack of care but misuse of power which wounds those who are hurting. You have probably heard the expression, "shooting the wounded." This term applies to the gross injustices which occur throughout the church in response to brokenness, woundedness and sin. It happens when the woman who leaves the abusive situation finds herself blacklisted from the church as a result of the divorce handed to her at the end of her traumatic ordeal. It happens when the man with the sexual addiction confesses his sin to leadership in hopes of finding support and healing, only to find himself stripped of his ministry position. It happens when the young woman discloses to her pastor that she has an eating disorder, and he makes her publicly confess her "sin" (in his estimation, her eating disorder) and removes her from volunteering with the youth. It happens when the widowed pastor marries a divorced woman and is stripped of his credentials and "relieved of his ministry duties." Or when the young couple who slips into sexual intimacy outside of marriage, ends up pregnant and turning to the church, finds condemnation and judgment. I think you get the idea, at least I hope you do.

"Shooting the wounded" is a response in which, the church, uneasy with its own fallen state, leans toward truth without grace. The results are devastating, and sometimes even fatal. Fatal wounding, mortal blow—however you phrase it, the end result can be physical, emotional or spiritual death at the hands of the ones we most expect to heal. What an opportunity we have as the body of Christ, to speak into peoples' lives when they are searching—faced with their own brokenness and need! Often we do okay with unbelievers, we expect them to sin and be affected by sin, but we tend to react differently to those in our own spiritual community. Our pride and self-righteousness kicks in, and we pull out our tweezers, hands trembling as we try to navigate around that blasted log in our own pathway of vision!

The problem is we're all broken! We live in a broken, fallen, sinful world that is under the management of Satan, as evidenced in Luke 4:6, "The Devil told him (Jesus), "I will *give you* the glory of these kingdoms and authority over them–because *they are mine* to give to anyone I please" (emphasis added). Three times in the Gospel of John, Jesus refers to Satan as "the ruler of this world (John 12:31, 14:30, 16:11)." Satan is an evil slum lord, exerting his authority on this earth, prowling "around like a roaring lion, seeking someone to devour (I Peter 5:8)." Those "someones" are us! Do not be naive about the spiritual war that is going on around us! This passage in I Peter was written to believers. I once had a patient who described her spiritual armor as weakened down to "a bottle cap for a shield and a toothpick for a sword." Let us be bold and strong, putting on the full armor of God (Eph. 6:10-18)! Verse 11 urges us to "stand firm against all strategies and tricks of the Devil." Sounds like a terrorist attack to me! Be wise!!

When life happens, sin happens, change happens - and we find ourselves under the weight of emotional, mental, spiritual and sometimes even physical struggle. This is the time when we most need the body of Christ, not a firing squad! I'm quite certain Satan is overjoyed when he hears that "cocking sound" coming from the steps of the church. Rather like the predatory animal, dividing the hurting animal from the rest of the herd.

The church needs to be less like the wildebeest, which runs frantically when attacked—every beest for himself—and more like the musk ox! For my non-Canadian friends who may have missed the awesome experience of learning about the musk ox (and being able to carve him out of a bar of soap in grade 3), allow me to educate you. The fascinating communal aspect of the musk ox is when the herd is attacked or threatened by a pack of wolves they form a circle around their calves, with the bulls and cows facing outward. Their large, powerful heads boast massive horns which fend off the attackers. (They've got to have something to compensate for their disproportionate heads, little ears and musky odour!)

How do we keep from shooting our wounded? The first step is to monitor our words and responses. One simple rule of thumb in discerning whether our words are in line with God, is to ask yourself whether you are speaking life or death into the situation or person. If the statements being made are life giving, then it is of God. If it is death giving and wreaks of the grave, it is not of God! Sometimes a judgmental remark, slipped in under the guise of humour, breeds just a fraction of death in someone's shame filled soul. We need to be cautious about how we react to the pain of other people, particularly our own Christian brothers and sisters. We must bring our thoughts captive before the Lord Jesus Christ, before speaking into the lives of someone else. What is our motive? Is it love? Is it a movement toward restoration and healing or is it just cold-hearted judgment resonating from our pharisaical soul? The church needs to be a place of safety in the midst of pain. There is a time and place for confronting sin, if present, but we've got to stop shooting the wounded as they come through the doorways of our churches!

A second step is to re-think and redefine our view of suffering! It's amazing how quickly we default to "Job's comforters," even after doing a study on the book of Job! On the whole, North American Christians are tremendously uncomfortable with the reality of suffering and pain. Century after century, we hear about the role of suffering, pain, trials, etc., and yet we long to believe something else. Our human nature balks at the sight of struggle. We sprawl and lunge, desperately trying to avoid the inevitable, like my cats when I lower them into their semi-annual bath in a warm tub filled with water! As our Hebrew ancestors, we have a lousy memory regarding God's faithfulness, and we forget both the reality of suffering and the possible benefits. As Larry Crabb says in his book "SoulTalk," "brokenness releases the holy passion lying dormant in the depths of our soul."[2] Sonic Flood sings a very poignant chorus (which is often skipped, like verse three of every hymn sung in a Baptist church), "Brokenness... brokenness, it's what I long for. Brokenness, it's what I need. Brokenness, brokenness, is what you want from me."

Oh don't worry, I've got some wonderfully positive examples of care too! My family was there for me, praise God! A big thank you to Mum and Dad! As well, my dear Bible study group from the church I attended before moving to the city was an awesome support to me. I could not have survived the initial struggles of separation, and it's concentric circles of devastation, without those loving women! I thank God for placing them in my life! Especially in the midst of a church environment that didn't handle my situation with grace! If I hadn't tasted the goodness of God prior to that time, I would certainly have left the church after the spiritual abuse, misuse of power and judgment I encountered.

Our ladies' group shared many a weeping session, crying out to God in prayer, as well as times of humour in the midst of it all (God has "gifted" me with an incredible wit that can find humour in the most difficult, and sometimes bizarre, times of life). Additionally, one of my dear friends lost her husband to cancer during that time, so we were thrown into a tumultuous time of scrambling for God. These ladies were a constant support, available to me by phone or in person, and we shared regular times of study, prayer, support and fun. Community! Caring community!

Another example of care during that first year of separation was when someone, who I still do not know to this day, played the "12 Days of Christmas" on us. We were heading into a desperately bleak Christmas. It was looking as though there wouldn't be any crutches for Little Timmy, and it was "the first" Christmas season alone. Some dear souls spent twelve days placing gifts on our doorstep and running for their lives! I got so that I could sprint from the back of the townhouse to the front door in 2.4 seconds, yet those Olympic Do-Gooders had me beat! (We also scared the odd person with how quickly we whipped the door open!) The generosity of those people, brought an incomparable spark to our family Christmas that year! My boys waited eagerly each day for the package to be delivered. It was an absolute visitation of God to our broken and wounded lives, at a time when we most needed strength and encouragement.

I must tell you of one other "care" episode that year. In my efforts to find a small group connection I called a different church in our area. I asked to speak to the person who was responsible for pastoral care in their church. A kind woman came on the line and asked me to describe what was going on in my life. After listening for a few minutes, she requested that I give her my address and phone number. *"Okay,"* I thought. We ended the conversation with her promise that she would see what she could do. Somewhat comforted by having been listened to, I went about my day. Suddenly the doorbell rang and a concerned looking woman introduced herself as being from the church I had just called. I soon discovered that even the simple disclosure of my present life circumstances was enough to have a pastor show up and do a suicide assessment! Tee hee! When I figured out why she had arrived so quickly, I started to laugh and assured her that, although my life was rather depressing, I was indeed safe and functional! In fact, she ended up staying for tea, and I sang her the song I had written out of my weakness. (She ended up crying, but fortunately did not become suicidal!)

These events planted seeds in me with regard to the church and care ministries. I experienced many exchanges with the church throughout my times of crisis, up to the present. Sometimes I found abundant care, the kind that makes you close your eyes and believe you have honestly looked into the face of God. Sometimes I discovered a tremendous lack of care, which prompted me to press on with the calling God had placed on my life. Other times, much to my horror, I encountered a cryptic avoidance of care ministries within the church. The coldness of which left me more determined to see that God's church—the body of Christ—be redeemed and restored as a caring community. As a Christian, I did not want to access secular counselling services and support, I just wanted to do my healing work under the care and direction of someone who believed in the healing power of God! What I found were waiting lists of up to a year for affordable counselling and a scarcity of Christian counselling, even at $120 per hour!

I was able to get the odd hour of counselling here and there, but only on a crisis basis. I am thankful that I was eventually able to obtain counselling from a female pastor at the Church of God, who had a counselling degree. She ended up waiving her hourly rates and walked me through some very dark times. I praise God for her willingness and her commitment to serve

God in this role! Thank you, Bev! As I met more Christians who had gone through difficult times, I heard the same recurring theme, "Christian counselling is inaccessible and unaffordable." "Why can't we get the help we need from the church?"

Therein lies the passion which has birthed this book. When I first started to write on the "crisis of care" in the church, I intended to write a magazine article. God was prompting me to begin the work shortly after I arrived home from an amazing conference in Vancouver. Beth Moore was the plenary speaker, and she spoke a powerful challenge to us as Christian women in leadership. Throughout the course of the weekend, God continued to impress on me the need to follow Him and obey Him, no matter what. It became clear that no obstacle should prevent me or distract me from opening my mouth when and where God nudges me to do so. I thought that was quite sufficient for one weekend! But no! God was STILL speaking! He wanted me to start writing, and to tackle the crisis of care within the Christian church.

I assured God that I was willing, but had no idea when I would find time for such a huge undertaking. Well, never tell God you don't have enough time (and never tell your intercessor friends that you want to be obedient!) I soon discovered that my late night hours—during which I could barely exist without sleep—were transformed into dynamic writing times! Not only were they productive, but I became so consumed with passion in pursuing what God was placing in my heart that I could scarcely log off my computer and go to bed!

So sit back, relax and pray your way through this book. In fact, before we go any further, would you give me the privilege of praying for you?

"Father God, use this book for Your glory, to incite change in Your Bride, the church, and her every believer. May my words be guided by You, and in alignment with what You would desire for an awakening in the church as a whole. May we become a body of radically obedient people who are truly needy and desperate for You. Fill us with Your Holy Spirit, and grant us a true understanding of what it means to be a caring community of believers. God, forgive me if I write anything that is not of You and in accordance with Your purposes for this work. Redeem it, and bring good of it for Your glory. "May the words of my mouth, and the meditations of my heart be pleasing to you oh God, my Rock and my Redeemer (Ps. 19:14)." In the mighty name of the Lord Jesus Christ, amen."

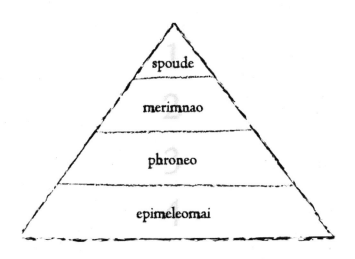

spoude

merimnao

phroneo

epimeleomai

In ancient Jewish culture, care and hospitality were virtually interchangeable and viewed as a central societal pillar. "For the people of ancient Israel, understanding themselves as strangers and sojourners, with responsibility to care for vulnerable strangers in their midst, was part of what it meant to be the people of God."[3] Jesus was dependent on the hospitality of those around Him, and was gracious in extending hospitality and care through His words and actions. As the church became established in the New Testament, the tradition of hospitality was taught as "a spiritual obligation…a dynamic expression of vibrant Christianity."[4] It was even a qualification for leadership in the early church, and a "fundamental expression of the gospel."[5] The Christian practice of hospitality carries a far broader meaning than is presently perceived, and was "understood to encompass physical, social, and spiritual dimensions of human existence and relationships."[6]

In the early years of the church, care was a primary focus of the believers. Ancient manuscripts outline the communal and caring nature of the church. "They joined together with the other believers and devoted themselves to the apostles' teaching and fellowship, sharing in the Lord's Supper and in prayer...the believers met together constantly and shared everything they had. They sold their possessions and shared the proceeds with those in need. They worshiped together at the Temple each day, met in homes for the Lord's Supper, and shared their meals with great joy and generosity—all the while praising God and enjoying the goodwill of all the people. And each day the Lord added to their group those who were being saved (Acts 2: 24-47)." Is it any wonder their numbers were increasing daily?! I can't even fathom seeing such a phenomenon in our modern-day culture!

People had things in common, were sharing and partaking of life together on a daily basis. The Book of Acts showed people who were culturally relevant—meeting the people where they were at, and shaping their outreach to meet the needs of each people group they encountered. In fact, their care extended throughout all of the Christian church, not just local churches. Throughout Paul's journeys, he was enlisting help from one church to another, as needs arose. In Acts 11, there is a great famine during the reign of Claudius. "So the believers in Antioch decided to send relief to the believers in Judea, everyone giving as much as they could (11:29)." In Philippians, Paul commends the church for giving to help meet his needs, and also for the offering they collected for the Jews.

Many church historians speak highly of the Christian practice of hospitality—which equates to the modern day practice of benevolence. Christian hospitality is not merely about having someone over for supper or giving someone a place to stay. As Christine Pohl, professor of Christian social ethics at Asbury Theological Seminary, states: "For the most part, the term "hospitality" has lost its moral dimension and, in the process, most Christians have lost touch with the amazingly rich and complex tradition of hospitality."[7] This fits into the discipline of the Christian life, as evidenced in systematic theology. The active practice of having a "disciplined Christian life is a sign of the true church."[8] The gist of which is, without Christian behaviour, there is no church. Where the true church is, there are people walking daily in the way of holiness—walking their talk. The sign of the true church includes "pastoral care of the members of the Church; the preserving of the pure doctrine through the exercise of spiritual discipline and the opposing of false doctrines; the doing of works of mercy."[9]

The requirements for the position of elder in the church include the regular practice of hospitality. When Paul writes to Titus (as he did to Timothy), he outlines the criteria for leadership. In chapter one, verse 8, Paul writes, "He must enjoy having guests in his home and must love all that is good." The criteria for elder and deacon are quite in-depth and target characteristics that make it easy to connect with a person. Most of our elders' boards are filled with people who have good skills, jobs and management capabilities, but do they possess the ability to connect with, and sincerely care for people? Larry Crabb proposes in his book "Connecting" that professional Christian counsellors might not even be necessary if elders were doing what God intended them to do. If godly elders are functioning as shepherds—displaying wisdom and spiritual discernment—then the work of the therapist should decrease! It appears that the same character and credentials that compel us to connect with a counsellor, are also what describe the church elder.[10]

Hospitality continues to be addressed in Matthew 25. Jesus spoke strongly in regard to the final judgment and the division of the sheep and the goats. He welcomed the group on His right hand, with a blessing from His Father, saying, "For I was hungry, and you fed me. I was thirsty, and you gave me a drink. I was a stranger, and you invited me into your home. I was naked, and you gave me clothing. I was sick and you cared for me. I was in prison, and you visited me (Matt. 25:35-36)." Wow, can you imagine actually being able to do those things for Christ?! To feed Him, give Him drink, have Him come over, visit Him and care for Him?! What an honour! Yet, the passage goes on to attend to the bewilderment of those being blessed. "But when did we do these things for you Lord?" asks the crowd. The response of the King assures them, "When you did it to one of the least of these my brothers and sisters, you were doing it to me! (Matt. 25:40)." I wish the passage ended there, but it goes on to attend to those who did not engage in acts of hospitality. The scriptures go on to declare that the refusal of such treatment is a refusal to help God, with the end result being eternal punishment, rather than eternal life (25:45-46). Gulp!

The compelling force behind care is love—agape love. C.S. Lewis calls agape, "gift love." "Agape is the love of God who, needing nothing, "loves into existence wholly superfluous creatures in order that He may love and perfect them."[11] It is the love that requires nothing in return. It brings the concern for others up to the level of caring for one's self. Agape is the kind of love spoken about in Matt. 22:39, when Jesus said, "Love your neighbor as yourself." In other words, allow the love of almighty God work in you and through you to sincerely care for others.

For me, agape love is the love that I sometimes can't explain. It is the kind of love that I have for another person without even knowing him or her. It hooks into compassion and mercy, and perhaps a glimpsing of God's hope for that person. I have felt incredible love on occasion for someone I didn't even know. Yet I could see the good in them, beyond their masks and facades. It was as though God was peeling their masks back and giving me a glimpse of who He created them to be. How could we not have love for someone, when we borrow the eyes of Christ to view them? One silly way that I remember the term "agape," is to use the Canadian translation, which is "a gap, eh?" God grants us love by which to fill in the gap, eh!? (Groan if you will, but you will probably have that painfully stuck in your memory for quite some time now!)

I John is perhaps the most consolidated look at what it means to love each other within the body of Christ. Love is described as the paramount feature and mark of having a true relationship with Christ. Chapter three, verse 10, puts it strongly, "So now we can tell who are children of God and who are children of the Devil. Anyone who does not obey God's commands and does not love other Christians does not belong to God."

From I John 2:5-5:3, there are 43 instances of the word "love" or "loving." Amazingly, all 43 uses are the same Greek word, *agapao*, which is the root word for agape. The specific nature of *agapao* is "to love (in a social or moral sense): comparative to *phileo*, to be a friend to: embracing especially the judgment and the deliberate assent of the will as a matter of principle, duty and propriety." *Phileo* is "chiefly of the heart" and *agapao* is chiefly "of the head."

Christian love isn't about loving those we "want" to love or those we determine to be most "lovable." The imperative restated throughout the letter of first John is to love other Christians. "If we love other Christians, it proves that we have passed from death to eternal life. But a person who doesn't love them is still dead...We know what love is because Christ gave up his life for us. And so we also ought to give up our lives for our Christian friends. But if one of you has enough money to live well, and see a brother or sister in need and refuses to help—how can God's love be in that person? Dear children, let us stop just saying we love each other; let us really show it by our actions (I John 3:14,16-18)." Keep in mind that the word for love throughout the book refers to a thoughtful befriending of someone—loving them in a social or moral sense. We have a duty to love other believers, period; to care for them and help meet their needs.

One of my more stretching classes at seminary was systematic theology. In one of these courses, we had the pleasure of reading Thomas C. Oden, "Life in the Spirit," Systematic Theology Volume Three. I still remember taking my boys to Cincinnati for their spring break and laying by the pool reading Oden! Yes, it did provide for some interesting looks and interactions. I learned a tremendous amount from that course, and that book in particular (it was just so long and complex!) Oden had much to say about the community of believers, the church. He defined Christian church as "the community through whom the Holy Spirit administers redemption and distributes gifts, the means in and by which God makes his reconciling work in Christ present to humanity...the church is the personal communion of those who have communion with the living Christ."[12] Yeah, let that soak in and imagine reading another 502 pages! Community, redemption, reconciliation, communion and the living Christ, sounds like a recipe for powerful transformation!

In order for the modern-day church to be effective, we have to look at our theology. What IS church? What is the theology of church? This was the subject of many early church meetings, councils, writings and edicts. What is the role and purpose of the church? Why do we exist? WHY does the body of Christ continue to exist throughout the centuries? WHAT is it supposed to look like? HOW does it get defined? I am going to touch briefly on a disconcerting trend that I see taking place in many churches. Sorry if I'm poking your sacred cow in the eye, but I can't help myself! There is a trend within church leadership circles toward incorporating secular business principles and ethics into the church. I've even heard it said, "The church is a business." This is a very precarious line for the church to be walking! Church is not corporate business! Can we learn some things from "corporate America?" Yes, just as we can learn from all aspects of society, but we cannot let the philosophies of secular society define the life and workings of the church.

One result of the secularization of church leadership and incorporation of corporate business models into the scope of the church is how it is affecting our hiring processes. I am meeting more and more people in full-time ministry who have fluid corporate skills and marketability, yet no sense of calling from God! YIKES! I could work full-time in the secular marketplace, but I have a call from God to be in ministry. It changes HOW I do my work, WHY I do my work, and why

I can't NOT do it! Those of you with a call know what I'm talking about! Romans 11:29 says, "For God's gifts and his call can never be withdrawn" or as the NIV translates "are irrevocable." Ponder the long range effect of hiring people based solely on marketplace skills and suitability. Don't get me wrong I'm entirely for professional standards within the church and excellence in ministry, but we had better have a call from God or we're going to be puffing along on our own steam!

The church is a transforming power, taking broken sinners and melding them with the power of the Holy Spirit through salvation and faith in Jesus Christ. This requires a bringing together of love and sin. In order to move sinners into salvation and a life of personal holiness, the church must love and come into close proximity with those they are commissioned to reach, save and sanctify. If you haven't heard the analogy of a church being a hospital, you need to envision the powerful metaphor of the local church being a "M.A.S.H." unit. "As in triage, those most desperately fallen are most urgently sought and cared for, as in the parable of the lost sheep. The church has repeatedly found in the most notorious sinners its most brilliant and winning advocates (from Mary Magdalene and Paul to Saint Francis and John Newton)."[13]

"Wait just a minute! Are you saying the church is supposed to be like some kind of medical centre? An emergency ward with bleeding, dying bodies?!" Yes, I am! The church must be a centre for healing. Where every sinner can come into the presence of Christ's functioning body here on earth (remember that sin is sin is sin—there is no hierarchy!) and receive care, healing, recuperation and transition into fullness of life. "But we don't want to target our ministry toward broken people, otherwise we will alienate the wealthy young businessman who "has all his ducks in a row." Firstly, we are all broken people! Say this with me, "I am a broken and sinful person, who without the grace of God, cannot possibly find redemption and forgiveness for my sins." Secondly, NOBODY's ducks matter the least when it comes to salvation and sanctification; in fact, our ducks can often "do things" that muddy the waters! The wealthy young businessman may have his externals well in place, and appropriate masks for the various occasions he faces, but he is just as broken by sin as the "crack" addict who has lost everything. The big difference is that one realizes their need for a Savior more quickly!

I didn't see Jesus pursuing the rich, young rulers of His day. In fact, scripture shows us a pretty hard line with regard to riches and their power to sway us from our need for God. Matthew 19 retells the confrontation between Jesus and the rich, young ruler. The young man is drawn by legalism, the rigidity of rules—which compliments his sense of control and influence. He wants to know which rules he needs to keep in order to gain eternal life. Discontent and well aware that legalism is not giving him fulfillment, he asks, "What do I still lack (vs. 20)?" Jesus tells him to sell what he has, give it to the poor, and follow Him in a life of obedience. What an awesome opportunity this young lad missed! To be able to ask Jesus the question, "What do I still lack?"

Can you imagine being able to ask Jesus one question, face to face like that?! "I know that I've been good! I do all the right things, give to the right charities, make wise choices and everything looks good. People think highly of me! I've done well for myself! My ducks are all in a row! And yet I know there is something missing! God, I have this void…how do I rid myself of this terrible, aching void?" "Here's how," replies Jesus, "shoot the duck! Let go of whatever is more important to you than Me." "But..." I can hear the arguments in my head, the rationalization, the minimization, the denial, the projection, the blame; on and on we go trying to convince God that He doesn't understand!

How many of us, like that rich young man, would go away sorrowful, not liking the response from our Lord? "Can't we just do all the right things?!? Why does it have to affect us so deeply, cost us so much?" Jesus goes on to say that it is harder for a rich man to enter the kingdom of heaven than it is for a camel to go through the eye of a needle (which I believe is actually the biblical reference to childbirth, but I digress!) (Matthew 19:23-24.) The disciples were discouraged by this sternness and pleaded with Jesus, "Who then can be saved (vs. 25)?" His response reminds us who the Source of salvation is, "With men this is impossible, but with God all things are possible (vs. 26)." Once again, we arrive at grace, not our own merit.

I love how Oden defines this dynamic of church life as "the incarnational paradox of the church's sanctity."[14] This incarnational paradox is that a Mediator who was without sin came to expunge us of our sins. It is the Sinless One, washing the feet of the sinners, walking into the midst of garbage in order to pull us out of our garbage. Christ was sinless, yet fully engaged with sinners. Similarly, the church must embrace sinners while being "at the same time holy and always in need of being purified...this does not diminish but intensifies the call of the church to holiness and mature embodiment of the life of love."[15] This transformational pattern of engaging with a hurting world is evidenced throughout the Book of Acts and centuries of church history—the church dancing with her Lord, being so cared for and loved that those standing on the sidelines want to cut in!

The Book of James also speaks about care. In chapter two, favouritism is forbidden! We are warned not to give special treatment based on appearance. "If you show special attention to the man wearing fine clothes and say, "Here's a good seat for you," but say to the poor man, "You stand there" or "Sit on the floor by my feet," have you not discriminated among yourselves and become judges with evil thoughts (James 2:3-4, NIV)?" James goes on to remind us of the command to "love your neighbour as yourself" and explains that faith without deeds is dead. This message takes an entire chapter in the book of James, and includes some fairly direct comments from the writer in regard to integrity. We can't profess true faith, and not follow through with acts of kindness and mercy! The important point is faith in Christ. It causes us—moves us—into action. If our faith is living, it continues to breed life.

When I was growing up, my Mum made these biscuits with "monster" dough. It was one of those fermented, yeast based mixes which was used to spawn further baking! If the "monster" wasn't used on a continual basis for baking, or given away to someone (so their children could be plagued with numerous "monster" baked goods!), the "starter batch" would become rancid. It had to be used! It could actually creep out of the top of a container, if no one was paying attention to it! The one thing I most vividly remember about the "monster" is what happened to it when it "went bad." It was the most vile, most disgusting-smelling and most disgusting-looking vat of batter you can imagine! The bowl in which it was contained was best just laid to rest with the remnants of the "monster!" I think it is similar with our faith. It has to be used!! It has to be given away to others! It has to be active, otherwise it will spoil and become useless. Not only useless, but vile and unusable, causing damage to the container.

In the Book of Acts, we see further acts of practical care. In chapter six, discontent rises among the church ranks with concern regarding care of the widows. The Greek believers "complained against those who spoke Hebrew, saying that their widows were being discriminated against in the daily distribution of food (vs. 1)." The Apostles' response? They called a meeting of all the believers and had the people select seven men, who were "well respected...full of the Holy Spirit and wisdom. We will put them in charge of this business (vs. 3.)" This "business" was part of the work of the church, to care for those in need, especially the widows.

It is interesting to note that the Greek word for widow, is *chera* (khay-rah); a feminine derivative from the word *chasma*, which means a "chasm" or vacancy, "through the idea of deficiency; a widow (as lacking a husband); literal or figurative, widow."[16] Recall for a moment the middle Eastern culture at that time. Those women without a husband had very little means to provide for themselves, other than prostitution. Thus it became part of the church's role to care for those without a husband, so they would not have to go into prostitution or slavery. This reality makes the church's movement towards care even more vivid and life-changing. One act of Christ's compassion and care was seen in Luke 7:11-15, when Jesus raised the widow's son from the dead. Not only did Christ restore the life of her only son, but He also gave her the gift of continued care and provision—preventing a life of prostitution or slavery! Now THAT's my kind of Saviour!

Questions to discuss and ponder.

1. What are your thoughts on the Christian tradition of hospitality?
2. Describe your own personal experience(s) of Christian hospitality.
3. List at least three ways you can personally build the practice of hospitality into your life.
4. What does *agapao* love look like in present-day terms?
5. What are some ways you can show *agapao* love to your friends, family, church and those you don't know?
6. What "ducks" of yours need to be shot? What is more important to you than your relationship with Christ?
7. Discuss the "incarnational paradox of the church's sanctity" and determine at least five ways you (and your church) can be incarnational in ministry to your community.
8. Think of some ways you can exercise your faith so it continues to grow.
9. Reflect on this chapter and the information presented. How do you better understand the need for care in the church?
10. Spend some time in prayer related to reclaiming the Christian tradition of hospitality and care for your local church body.

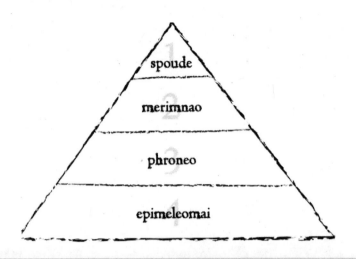

spoude

merimnao

phroneo

epimeleomai

CULTURAL RELEVANCE OF THE CHURCH

The Apostle Paul said, "I have become all things to all men, so that I may by all means save some (I Cor. 9:22)." This became wonderfully pronounced as I stood in the excavation site of Ephesus, listening to my Muslim guide describe how culturally relevant Paul was in furthering the gospel! Throughout that study tour, I had Turkish and Greek guides (who did not share my faith and therefore had no vested interest or bias) explain what some of the New Testament scriptures meant, in their full cultural context. For example, in Paul's first letter to Timothy (2:9), he says that women ought not to wear their hair braided up on top of their heads. Why? To be legalistic and establish a human law? No, because the prostitutes of that time and culture wore their hair up in braids on top of their heads. That was part of their advertising scheme! We even saw a foot stone where the graphics portrayed the message, "For the love of a good woman, walk this way." The woman had hair piled up in braids on her head. The message of scripture being, "don't succumb to societal standards of beauty which might get you confused with being a prostitute!"

Another piece of interesting history was found in the ruins of Corinth. We saw phenomenal pillars at the temple, ancient Roman baths, the Bema seat of judgment, and impressively preserved sculptures. (One had no arms or a head, so I struck my pose strategically behind it, citing, "Friends, Romans, Countrymen, lend me your ears, for I have none!) In our touring, we discovered the Agora—the marketplace, and the butcher shop. Interestingly, the butcher shop was located kitty-corner from the temple of Apollos. A hop, skip and a jump to ship the sacrificial meat over to the deli for re-sale. Hmmm, could that have been why Paul was so quick to address the problem of eating meat which had been offered to idols? Yes, another instance of cultural relevance! The cultural pattern of the people was to bring their gifts and sacrifices, including meat, and offer them to their gods at the temple. The meats were then sold at the local meat shop. (The Corinthian "Subway" was not yet in operation!)

Cultural relevance is also seen in how Paul interacts with various people groups. When in Athens (Acts 17), Paul delivers a pivotal message on Mars Hill. He meets the people where they are at, spiritually. He pays attention to the culture around him, noting the Athenians have an altar to "an unknown god." Paul uses that description as an opening to share the gospel with a very astute crowd of philosophers and intellectuals who were not open to the gospel in the ways it was shared in Israel and parts of Asia Minor. Jews often looked for signs, but Greeks and Romans wanted logical arguments. Further on, in Acts 22, Paul addresses the crowd in Jerusalem after his arrest. He chooses to speak to the crowd in their own language, Aramaic. The text goes on to say, "When they heard him speaking in their own language, the silence was even greater (22:2.)"

All that to say this—Paul was culturally relevant! The Apostle John was also culturally relevant! This theme came up again and again, as my feet walked across the archaeological sites of Asia Minor (Turkey), Greece and Patmos. Taking a look at our society, there is definitely reason to re-assess how to be culturally relevant in this new millennium! Oden reports on the defining marks of the *ekklesia* (those who are called out, or called together),[17] which is the church. One of these marks is the contradiction of being in the world and not of it. "The *ekklesia* is called to become fully humbled so as to take on earthly form, adapt itself to the temporal sphere, in order that it may fulfill its mission within and for the world, while yet not becoming indebted to the world."[18] Oden expands on this concept, "Where brokenness is found in the world, the church mends, where hunger, it feeds, where suffering, it assuages."[19]

So what happens when the church is not culturally relevant? If the church becomes irrelevant in our society, there is spiritual blindness and apathy. The Bride of Christ is not known among the non-believers, and the continued representation of Christ, here and now, is lost from sight. Thomas Merton writes, "In the whole world, throughout the whole of history, even among religious men and among saints, Christ suffers dismemberment. His physical Body was crucified by Pilate and the Pharisees; His mystical Body is drawn and quartered from age to age by the devils in the agony of that disunion which is bred and vegetates in our souls, prone to selfishness and to sin."[20] What a powerful image, to dismember the body of Christ! He continues, "as long as we are on earth, the love that unites us will bring us suffering by our very contact with one another, because this love is the resetting of a Body of broken bones."[21] What a vivid illustration of how we can harm, and heal the body of Christ!

Walter Rauschenbusch, a recognized leader in the social gospel movement (late 1800's), wrote this in regard to the role of the church in society. "The demoralization of society…ought to appeal most powerfully to the Church, for the Church is to be the incarnation of the Christ-spirit on earth, the organized conscience of Christendom. It should be swiftest to awaken to every undeserved suffering, bravest to speak against every wrong, and strongest to rally the moral forces of the community against everything that threatens the better life among men."[22] Historically speaking, one of the primary dynamics of the church in North America, was to offer social related services to the people. The church was the center of education—including the first colleges and universities, support, fellowship, community and care. If you needed help, you knew you could go to the church. Prior to the establishment of regional governments, the church paved the way for settling the new frontiers of Canada and the United States. Church doors were never locked. Churches were known to be a place of refuge.

One way that we have lost our cultural relevance, is through the transitioning of care out of the church and into the hands of government and other social service agencies. The care that was once part and parcel of the church in North America, has become distinctly severed. The same Christian practice of hospitality which birthed social work, hospitals, hospices and hostels, has been delegated to the civic and domestic spheres.

Christine Pohl outlines the long-term consequences of this displacement of care, "The public and civic dimensions of hospitality... became detached from their Christian roots as the public sphere was increasingly secularized. At the same time, the domestic sphere became more privatized; households became smaller, more intimate, and less able or willing to receive strangers."[23] This de-centralization of care has also taken place within the walls of the church, with many pastors stating they "don't do pastoral care or personal appointments" as it is not their role.

Larry Crabb cites an intriguing insight from one of the prominent voices in the field of psychology, C.G. Jung: "that modern psychotherapy arose partly in response to the void in Christian community left by the Protestant insistence on private confession." Crabb goes on to enlighten us, "We no longer struggle together with our deepest concerns and our most internal battles...we rarely share in a way that requires the gospel for the community to survive and for meaningful bonding to occur. The masks remain in place; we tell only parts of our stories...when we feel the need for richer connection, we unburden ourselves with a therapist."[24] Confession has been excommunicated from the modern-day church, and therefore, secularized. How do we confess in a world that clings to "values free" and humanistic beliefs? If we are innately good, and there is no absolute truth, then why would there be anything to confess? Thus we live in a prison of shame and secrecy, breeding a healthy diet for eating disorders, addiction and depravity—playing right into Satan's strategic attack of isolation.

I'm not saying the church needs to recapture the practice of public confession, or reallocate the social service system and reclaim every hospital, agency, and hospice for its own. My concern is what has happened to the church as a result of this shift! Even now, churches lament about what to do with all the broken people, secretly wishing they'd just go away! We don't want to offer counselling or get into the whole mental health "thing." Support groups, counselling centres, therapy, and recovery groups make us uneasy. "But Beth, those things are logistical and liability nightmares!" Oh yes, the arguments are many and varied! Liability issues, busy lifestyles, the clientele that such programs draw to the church (oh come on, be honest!), lack of volunteers, the financial costs, the small group movement—which attempts to decentralize care away from the church office, etc., etc.

Don't get me wrong, I'm all for small groups, but I believe we need to re-examine our concept of care. Small groups should be our first contact for primary care. Being plugged into a small group gives a person a microcosm of community. It is a place where we can know others and be known by them. Small groups offer an expanding network of care as they multiply. To be a part of a small group, gives you a life rope—a connection—to the larger church. Small group members encountering crisis have a "first call" contact in place to obtain support. A healthy group offers care, growth, accountability, practical assistance when needed, and referral to professionals when necessary.

I recently had the displeasure of having sinus surgery. I won't go into detail, other than to give you a visual involving a roto-rooter and a couple of industrial strength, ultra-absorbent plugs shoved up my nose! In the midst of recovering from this wonderful endeavour, during which time I was not to lift anything heavier than a phonebook, I discovered that I had an infestation of carpenter ants in my newly acquired home!

(Carpenter ants are the Canadian version of termites, only they belong to a union and wear little bitty tool belts and hard hats!) In order for the exterminator to "take care" of my little friends, everything in the house had to be moved six inches away from the wall, ceiling tiles had to be removed in the basement, light switches and face plates had to be removed, etc. Well, I don't know about you, but my furniture weighs much more than a phonebook! My first call was to my good friends who are also in my small group (coincidence?) They came out the next day and took my house apart, then came back a day later and put it all back together; the hands of Jesus, working effectively through the community of small groups!

However, there are limitations to small groups and their role in care ministry. Sometimes the need is too great for the small group to bear alone. Sometimes the need lies outside of the competence of the leadership of the group, at which time referral to appropriate professionals is essential. The small group is an excellent venue, and the first point of entry for an individual to receive care. The second point of entry, is the area of care at the church. Pastoral care, counselling, crisis intervention, and referral/resourcing are all aspects of what the church can offer. If your church is too small to support all levels above, it is still essential for the church to be familiarized with pastoral care and counselling, and have basic training in managing crisis. Why? Because crisis happens, and it will happen in your congregation!

One major disappointment I encountered in my Bible college and seminary training was the lack of pastoral care/counselling courses that were required for those headed into full-time ministry! Colleges and seminaries (and denominations) need to implement care-related courses into their basic requirements for ministry and ordination. Minimally, pastors need to have a basic understanding of mental health and crisis, so they are competent to assess the needs of people who come to them, and make appropriate referrals.

Think on this question for one entire minute, if bringing people to Christ became a liability issue, would we still do it? (Don't read on, unless you've spent a minute on that question!) I believe this is truly an issue where we are to be wise as serpents and gentle as doves (Matt. 10:16). As long as we are living out the gospel of Christ, we will meet opposition and be offensive to some. Let us never quit! Let us never back down from opposition or soften the message of the gospel so that truth disintegrates and we become utterly useless. In his book, "Grace and Truth, a Paradox" Randy Alcorn challenges us to revive rightful Christian living and Biblical balance—truth AND grace. It's a dialectic! A dialectic is when two terms seem to contradict when in fact both are true. For example, free will is both blessing and curse; I call it the terror of free will. Alcorn writes, "Instead of the world's apathy and tolerance, we offer grace. Instead of the world's relativism and deception, we offer truth. If we minimize grace, the world sees no hope for salvation. If we minimize truth, the world sees no need for salvation."[25]

As our culture continues to spiral out of control, and be led by the "man of lawlessness," we are going to see increased numbers of "broken people." We are in the end times, my friend! It will not get better before the return of Christ. Let me say it again, it will not get better before the return of Christ! "In the last days there will be very difficult times. For people will love only themselves and their money. They will be boastful and proud, scoffing at God, disobedient to their parents, and ungrateful. They will consider nothing sacred. They will be unloving and unforgiving; they will slander others and have no self-control; they will be cruel and have no interest in what is good. They will betray their friends, be reckless, be puffed up with pride and love pleasure rather than God. They will act as if they are religious, but they will reject the power that could make them godly (II Timothy 3:1-5.)" Hmmm, maybe that's what happens when the church loses its cultural relevance.

In light of this prophetic foretelling of the end times, we ought not be surprised by the increasing levels of dysfunction, brokenness and woundedness we are seeing! Even as recently as five years ago, most people had basic life skills and a frame of reference of what "health" looked like. More recently, we are encountering person after person, who has been raised not only in a total faith void, but without even the notion of what emotional, mental and sometimes physical health looks like. In my private practice, I am seeing more and more individuals who are 20 and 30 + years old, who do not even possess basic life skills. It used to be that the work of the church was fairly straight forward, to preach an evangelical message which led to salvation, disciple the individual and facilitate their transition into a life of service.

This "three step" of salvation, sanctification and service, is no longer working like it used to. Why? Because our culture has changed it's shape, and our churches need a paradigm shift! These people don't just need Jesus, they need an entire education regarding sanctification, and personal healing/deliverance and wholeness, possibly even basic life skills. It truly is in line with the fulfillment of Isaiah's prophecy in 61:1, "He has sent me to comfort the brokenhearted, and to announce that captives will be released and prisoners will be freed...to all who mourn...

he will give beauty for ashes, joy instead of mourning, praise instead of despair (61:1-3)."

Paul Tournier, renowned Swiss physician and psychiatrist, prescribes the Gospel as a healing message. In his book, "The Whole Person in a Broken World," Tournier speaks about the task of the church, and its need for transformation. "Our age is suffering because of the rift between the spiritual and the temporal. It is suffering not only because of the despiritualization of the world, but also because of the disincarnation of the church. The church...has separated itself from real life and thus simply abandoned the world to its practical difficulties and taken refuge in an ivory tower. And for this it bears a heavy responsibility for our present crisis."[26] Interestingly enough, these words were written in 1947 and translated into English in 1964!

I recently heard a song by a group called "Casting Crowns." They have a song on their self-titled album called, "If We Are The Body." It is based on James 2:1-9 and I John 5:19-21, and goes like this:

"It's crowded in worship today
As she slips in trying to fade into the faces
The girls teasing laughter is carrying farther than they know
Farther than they know

Chorus:

But if we are the body
Why aren't His arms reaching?
Why aren't His hands healing?
Why aren't His words teaching?

And if we are the body
Why aren't His feet going?
Why is His love not showing them there is a way?
There is a way.

A traveler is far away from home
He sheds his coat and quietly sinks into the back row
The weight of their judgmental glances
Tells him that his chances are better out on the road

Chorus:

Jesus paid much too high a price
For us to pick and choose who should come
And we are the body of Christ

Chorus:

Jesus is the way."

As part of my work, I am on contract (as of this writing) with a large church as their "Director of Care Ministries." One of my responsibilities is to oversee what they call "Pastor of the Day" or POD. The Pastor of the Day serves a half-day shift once a week, to deal with walk-ins or phonecalls which are care-related. Sometimes the requests are purely benevolent in nature, people needing assistance for groceries in the form of food vouchers, or bus tickets to get around the city. Sometimes the requests are purely spiritual in nature, people wanting to have their questions answered. When the financial need is great, we refer to our benevolent committee, and sometimes they are able to help with an unpaid bill or a security deposit. For the most part, the calls and walk-ins are from people who don't even attend the church but word gets around on the street! Whether the request is physically-need related or spiritual/emotional in nature, the opportunity is the same. We have the opportunity to provide pastoral care to these people. On occasion we have the privilege of sharing the gospel with them and seeing them come to Christ! We try to pray with the person and tell them about our services, inviting them to come back on the weekend.

This summer we saw an increase in POD calls. The need is growing! In speaking with other churches across the country, they are finding a similar trend. With government cut-backs and increasing costs of living, many people are facing impossible situations. This is an opportunity for us as the church, to make an impact. I find it disheartening that some people who cover POD-related requests at churches do their shift reluctantly and with a hint of disdain for those who are "bothering them." They'd rather be spending their time on other things. Their compassion quotient is minimal. It troubles my soul when I hear about such calls being handled poorly, with little regard and respect to the person in need. Oh God, forgive us! Help us to see these people with eyes of compassion and speak gently, respectfully into their lives. As the song by Casting Crowns says, "If we are the body..." why aren't we grabbing onto the opportunity to reach, teach, help, heal and show the power of God?

I recently discovered a passage from the Old Testament that doesn't sit well with my modern soul. It is Ezekiel 16:49, "Now this was the sin of your sister Sodom: She and her daughters were arrogant, overfed and unconcerned; they did not help the poor and needy. They were haughty and did detestable things before me. Therefore I did away with them as you have seen." Gulp! I was far more comfortable with my Sunday School understanding of what happened to Sodom! Sexual depravity made sense to me! Those guys in Sodom got down right nasty! Didn't they deserve to get wiped out?! Yet here, we see that sexual depravity was a product—a result of sin. Pride, complacency and apathy were the sins that led to Sodom's slippery slope. The precursor to the destruction of Sodom, was the sin of not caring for the poor and needy. What does that say to us today?!

We desperately need the renovating work of the Holy Spirit as we live the new life we have in Christ. In Colossians Paul tells us that the evil nature must be stripped away, and in it's place we have been clothed with a new nature "that is continually being renewed, as you learn more and more about Christ, who created this new nature within you (3:10.)" Another word for renewed is renovated! Jesus is renovating our lives! Praise God, take out that sledge hammer, call in the "Trading Spaces" angels, and do an extreme make-over on this soul!! As we go through this process of renovation, we are told that the "most important piece of clothing...is love. Love is what binds us all together in perfect harmony. And *let* the peace that comes from Christ rule in your hearts. For as members of one body you are called to live in peace. And always be thankful (3:14-15, emphasis mine.)"

Let's just review those verses in Colossians. We are being renewed or renovated as we mature in Christ. His working and teaching in our lives, is creating our new nature. In the midst of our sanctification (for that is what this renovating work is called in proper church lingo!), we are to put on love like a coat, to be outfitted in love. Love creates community. It breeds harmony. Do you remember that chorus we used to sing in church that went like this, "love, love, love, love, the gospel in a word is love. Love thy neighbour as thy brother, love, love, love." What if we actually believed this? A belief system dictates behaviour. It dictates thought content, and it affects how we feel. When we have a core belief system where the gospel is love, then our actions, thoughts and feelings will be love-based. Will we always "feel" loving? No, but maybe, just maybe, our motives will be guided by love, rather than indifference or self-centeredness.

To conclude this chapter, reflect on these thoughts by Tournier. If we want to "cure the world of its neurosis of defiance, if we believe that this is possible, if we mean to put an end to the deep disharmony of modern life, if we are to help men become whole in a broken world, if we are seeking the way to a culture in which all the disciplines are inspired by God, we do so because he himself is calling us to this task. As in the days of the prophets his voice is raised above the ruins."[27]

Questions to discuss and ponder...

1. Discuss the need for the church to be culturally relevant.

2. What are the "marks" of the church being culturally relevant? How is your church culturally relevant (or not)?

3. Think of ways to improve the cultural relevance of your local church (brainstorm and write down at least four practical actions which would increase the cultural relevance of your church.) Think outside the box! Get creative!

4. How can small groups ensure cultural relevance?

5. Discuss changes you have seen regarding increasing levels of dysfunction, brokenness and woundedness.

6. What have you witnessed as effective in working with these changes? (If nothing, brainstorm ideas which may help.)

7. Why is the balance between grace and truth so essential?

8. List three aspects of your life that you want the Holy Spirit to renovate—are you willing to pray along those lines and have a friend hold you accountable?

9. How do you respond emotionally to scriptures like Matthew 25 and Ezekiel 16:49 which point out the necessity of caring for the poor and needy?

10. What is one change you can make in how you spend your time, money, energy or prayers related to the issue of cultural relevance?

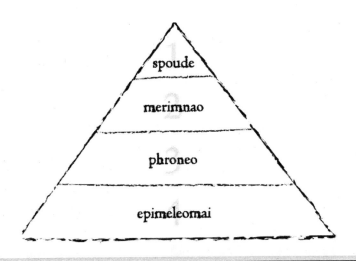

spoude

merimnao

phroneo

epimeleomai

TRANSFORMATIONAL DISCIPLESHIP

You've probably gathered that I am going somewhere with all this (at least I hope you have)! What I'm proposing is this, a concept I call "transformational discipleship." It's a twinning of the discipleship step, which acknowledges the complicating factors we are now facing. The "three step" becomes more of a "four step," if you will. Salvation, sanctification AND an intentional healing process, to enable the convert to transition successfully into a life of service. Instead of simply teaching Biblical education and spiritual truths, we must also teach, counsel and attend to the issues which require more intense healing, prayer ministry and/or deliverance. (Interestingly, accounts of church history reveal deliverance as being a normal part of the conversion process.)

In Mark, chapter four, Jesus tells the parable of the sower. The sower throws his seed, and it lands on four different types of ground: the path, rocky ground, where there are thorns, and in the good soil. Of the seeds on the path, Jesus says Satan comes immediately and takes away the word that was sown in them. For the rocky ground, there is a receiving with joy, but there is insufficient rooting available, and any affliction causes them to "fall away." The good soil gives the seed a strong foundation and reaps a bountiful harvest. It is the thorny ground that catches my attention in regard to transformational discipleship. Mark 4:18-19 reads, "And others are the ones on whom seed was sown among the thorns; these are the ones who have heard the word, but the worries of the world, and the deceitfulness of riches, and the desires for other things enter in and choke the word, and it becomes unfruitful (NASB)."

The Greek word for "enter in" is *eisporeuomai* (ice-por-yoo-om-ahee) and in this case, it is a metaphor of "affections entering the soul."[28] The word for choke is *sumpnigo* (soom-pnee-go) and means to "choke utterly, metaphorically, the seed of the divine word sown in the mind, or to press round or throng one so as to almost suffocate him."[29] Hang in there for one more Greek word, *akarpos* (ak-ar-pos), which is the word for unfruitful. *Akarpos* metaphorically means "without fruit, barren, not yield what it ought to yield."[30] It's all Greek to me, but when you really understand what this verse is saying, it is life-changing! The seeds among the thorns are the ones I believe we are losing in the three step process. They receive the seed of God but are still living amongst the prickly and painful reality of thorns. The worries (which is the Greek word *merimna*, for care, or anxiety through the idea of distraction) of our past and present realities utterly choke this divine word out of our minds.

The deceitfulness of riches and desires for other things, or as the King James states it, "lusts" for other things, consume our minds, passions and energy. The Greek word for riches here applies to "an abundance of external possessions; fulness, abundance, plenitude, or a good with which one is enriched."[31] Sounds an awful lot like addiction, doesn't it?? These clamoring forces choke out the new voice speaking truth into our mind, and screams a selfish demand for gratification, usually instant! The word for lust or desire here, carries an unhealthy, "forbidden fruit" kind of craving. The worries, the riches, the desires, they are all self-absorbed and narcissistic in nature. It's no wonder they crowd out the space in the mind where the good seed has fallen!

You've no doubt heard phrases like "the battlefield of the mind," "wrestling not with flesh and blood" and "taking every thought captive before the Lord Jesus Christ." This is reflective of what happens in the process of "choking." God's divine word is planted in the mind, where it is attacked by the thorns, which try to smother the new thoughts being evoked by God's Word. Our old messages kick in, our myths and distorted thinking pair up and influence our decision to accept the truth exuding from this new source. This new seed says I am lovable, acceptable, complete and forgiven. This new seed offers me unlimited growth potential! But those thorns! Those feelings of being inadequate, inferior, incomplete, unlovable and defective, they enter my soul and "choke utterly" the new beliefs that are growing in me. The end result is that I am unfruitful. I may survive, but I am not living the kind of life that I am meant to, I am not "yielding what I ought to yield."

In her most recent book, "When Godly People do Ungodly Things," Beth Moore tackles issues related to how seductive Satan's massive attacks are on the present-day church. She points out that people cannot get through the process of redemption and healing without other believers. Moore also emphasizes the need for a paradigm shift in this area, "this point is where good, godly counselling comes in as well as solid Bible study and a fuller understanding of a through-and-through kind of sanctification."[32] She goes on to explain a process of "detoxification, deprogramming and reprogramming"[33] for a believer who has been misled/seduced subtly by Satan, and is coming back into restored, Christian living. Have you been privy to working with someone who is coming out of some pretty bad stuff? They need to detoxify—that is, be physically, emotionally, spiritually and mentally purged of the toxin. Their faulty thinking needs to be challenged (deprogramming) and replaced with truth (reprogramming). From a cognitive-behavioral perspective, this is called thought stopping and replacement. From a Christian perspective, it is called the "renewing of your mind."

Due to the nature, and acuity of the levels of brokenness and dysfunction we are seeing in this generation, we must include a further dynamic of care. For example, a young business man who comes to salvation in his thirties, with a long history of sexual addiction, and alcohol/drug use, needs more than a Bible study! Don't miss what I'm saying here! Yes, he needs the Bible study! He needs to become intimately acquainted with the word of God, and develop a habit of intensive Bible reading and study. He also needs a mental and emotional study, in which he can address his prominent, long standing issues related to sexual issues, alcohol and drugs. "Can God not just heal these things?" Absolutely, and sometimes He does! Unfortunately, He often allows us to travel those long roads back home, and walk through the river of pain into healing.

These times offer incredible learning and insight about self and God. They develop character and perseverance, conforming us to the likeness of Christ.

I think this gives us a three-fold purpose: to truly know the healing power and comfort of God in our own lives, to comfort those who have comforted us, and to learn from our sufferings. "He (God) is the source of every mercy and the God who comforts us. He comforts us in all our troubles so that we can comfort others. When others are troubled, we will be able to give them the same comfort God has given us. We are confident that as you share in suffering, you will also share God's comfort (II Cor. 1:3-7.)" Several verses throughout the New Testament reveal that Christ suffered, and learned through his sufferings. If this was true for the Lord Jesus Christ, it is certainly more so true for us!

So, how do we reach a culture that is self-absorbed, corrupt, Godless, prideful and hurting? Can we really rely on the tried and true methods of the 20th century, or do we need to adapt? The levels of personal depravity and societal corruption have been deeply infected in the past 100 years. Institutions that once lauded the public praise and worship of God, have given way to "tolerance" and separation of church and state. Hospitals, hospices and mental health agencies have separated from the influence of the church. Absolute truth has become offensive to those who would rather philosophize about the idolatry of defining oneself as "God." The term "values free" has become a catch phrase in mental health settings. "Values free" service from psychologists, teachers, social workers, health care workers, counsellors and others, has translated into generations of truth seeking, rootless people who have no frame of reference for right and wrong. In saying there is no absolute truth, no values systems, we have sold our birthright, and are suffering the dire consequences of doing so as a society!

I would propose that in order to reach this culture, we must become relevant! We must re-assess our approach to evangelism and discipleship. Our outreach programs need to include a normalizing of struggle which offers the hope of a changed life. One such example is to offer studies on pertinent social and mental health issues such as depression, addiction, anxiety, stress and grief. To offer support groups and therapy groups related to the issues that flow out of the levels of brokenness in our society: gambling, sexual addiction, eating disorders, divorce recovery, alcohol and drug addiction, perfectionism, abuse recovery, self-hatred, grief, depression, anxiety, etc. If you're reading this and thinking, "yeah, but I don't have any problems like these," consider that every human being has suffered a severed relationship with God prior to salvation, and therefore has areas of his/her life that have been affected by sin. They may be old messages, a blurred image of who you are in Christ, generational baggage, a critical spirit, pride, or spiritual leprosy, where you feel nothing for God. Either way, we are all in need of the redemptive, restorative work of the Holy Spirit.

So, am I saying that the blood of Jesus and His sanctifying work in us is not sufficient?! BY NO MEANS! Jesus' saving grace is sufficient! His work on the cross is complete, and we are completely saved through our belief in Jesus Christ. "For God so loved the world, that He gave His only Son, so that everyone who believes in him will not perish but have eternal life (John 3:16)." Salvation is not the issue. Sanctification is not the issue. Please hear me on this, God's work of salvation and sanctification is completed by God, through His Holy Spirit for our redemption. It's a done deal, and not even our deal, but the working of God in us, and in cooperation with His Spirit.

The issue is cultural relevance and being the full and effective body of Christ as His church. God chooses to work in this world through us. (Not a wise choice, as far as I'm concerned, but nonetheless, it is His decision!) God chooses to include us in His work here on earth. He gives us free will, choices, and the opportunity for relationship—at whatever level of intimacy we choose. It is humbling and horrifying to see it as Dutch Sheets explains in "Intercessory Prayer," "So complete and final was God's decision to do things on earth through human beings that it cost God the Incarnation to regain what Adam gave away."[34]

Beth Moore puts it succinctly, "If we don't take Christ up on the fullness of joy and satisfaction within our walls, we are still subject to longing glances at life outside our walls."[35] Hence, the voids, the addictions, unfulfilled longings and sense of incompletion. We need transformational discipleship which utterly floods us with the reality that our sense of completion is found entirely and solely in Jesus Christ! He alone completes us! We see this flip-side in Colossians 2:8-10, when Paul warns us, "Don't let anyone lead you astray with empty philosophy and high-sounding nonsense that come from human thinking and from the evil powers of this world, and not from Christ. For in Christ the fullness of God lives in a human body, and you are complete through your union with Christ."

I see empty philosophy and high-sounding nonsense on a regular basis! It's in the newspaper and magazines, on television, and flowing out of the mouths of family, friends and strangers. Advice for "effective living" comes freely from the pop culture gurus—Dr. Phil, Oprah, and others. Yet one crucial piece is missing. Completion! All the external appearance factors in the universe can't do it! Financial security can't do it! The God-shaped vacuum, the hole, the void in our souls, can ONLY and rightly be filled by God Himself. God created the space for Himself, and waits patiently for us to invite Him in to satisfy the longing and desire for His presence. Our completion, our perfection is not about what we do, it is about Jesus Christ and His uniting with us. What a relief! It's not up to me to perfect myself! Romans 12 also speaks to us in regard to transformation, "Don't copy the behavior and customs of this world, but let God transform you into a new person by changing the way you think. Then you will know what God wants you to do, and you will know how good and pleasing and perfect his will really is (12:2)."

Many of the staff from our church just attended a leadership conference. It was hosted by a Christian organization, and promoted as being a high-level training conference for Christian leaders. An area of concern for me with this conference was that a number of the presenters were not Christian. They were teaching Christians and providing them marketable skills, but they were not Christian people. On the surface this may seem entirely plausible. These people are very successful at what they do. They have incredible skills, are well known, and are able to motivate others. They are leaders in their business fields and have compiled many accolades. I know of another such speaker. He is extremely successful, has built a vast empire and has a huge following. He's incredibly well known, able to motivate others, and has amazing skills. He is probably the best salesman of all time! No, it's not Donald Trump, but he does use the same quote, "You're fired!"—only his fire reeks of brimstone. His name is Satan!

I Corinthians 3:18-19 warns, "Do not deceive yourselves. If any one of you thinks he is wise by the standards of this age, he should become a 'fool' so that he may become wise. For the wisdom of this world is foolishness in God's sight." There are other scriptures including those earlier in this chapter, which speak to this issue about seeking wisdom from the world and looking to copy behaviour, customs, and philosophies of those who are non-believers. I don't see any accounts of the Apostle Paul inviting Caesar to come and speak to his new churches about a Roman leadership plan. The early church never looked to their culture to define the interior workings of the church, they looked to God for His leadership and definition. The Apostle John tells us to not love the world or anything from it (I John 2:15). Paul warns Timothy, "Guard what has been entrusted to your care. Turn away from godless chatter and the opposing ideas of what is falsely called knowledge, which some have professed and in so doing have wandered from the faith (I Tim. 6:20)."

"Can't we just glean and learn from these secular leaders?" Perhaps we can, but do we really have to go to the world in search of how to do things within the walls of the church? The Bible gives us clear direction of where we should look for wisdom and knowledge. "The wisdom that comes from heaven is first of all pure. It is also peace loving, gentle at all times, and willing to yield to others. It is full of mercy and good deeds. It shows no partiality and is always sincere. And those who are peacemakers will plant seeds of peace and reap a harvest of goodness (James 3:17-18)." Sounds like the best resource for wisdom that is available to us! I'm not saying there is nothing for us to learn from secular sources, but in regard to the work of the church and ministry related issues, we need to look to God and His resources, including the leaders He has raised up. This is especially important with regard to counselling, pastoral care and "spiritual care," as secular resources in this regard present many principles contrary to the Word of God.

On a more sobering note, the writer goes on to say, "You adulterers! Don't you realize that friendship with this world makes you an enemy of God? I say it again, that if your aim is to enjoy this world, you can't be a friend of God (4:4)." Adulterers?! Isn't that a little extreme, James?! I can understand an encouraging spiel to watch your level of engagement with the world, but adulterers?! This requires that we understand what adultery really means. Adultery isn't just about sexual infidelity, it means to be doubly-bonded. Since we are created for a single-bond relationship, we suffer consequences if we become bonded with two people/things at the same time. Bonding is a process that takes time and develops as levels of trust, intimacy and commitment increase. Just as we can't truly love, commit and invest in a marriage and be bonded to someone else, neither can we be emotionally and spiritually bonded to the world, and be bonded fully to God.

I realize I've probably stepped on a few toes with these last few paragraphs, and for that I am sorry. For the content of the paragraphs, I am not sorry. We must be ever so careful in our examination of what we allow into our church leadership and ministry, that it be from God, and not man! This brings me back to the issue of calling that I stated earlier in the book. Those of us with a call know the gnawing, compelling need to obey God, and follow His direction. (If you're not certain whether you have a call, just try not to do it! If you can put it aside and live peacefully, it's not a calling! If you can't NOT do it, you have a calling!) His direction doesn't always make sense, look rational or line up with our feelings—although it will always resonate with our spirit. If we look outside of the circle of believers for training and instruction, we are at risk of being subtly led away from God's direction and will. Let us not look to empty philosophy and high-sounding nonsense from this world!

A few years ago, I was doing a chapel presentation on completion, using the verses in Colossians as stated above. I love to use video clips and songs to help bring the point home (and to help the ADHD people in the crowd!) I looked long and hard for a song about how Christ completes us, how his love fills that void that we have, and I didn't find anything! So I asked God for a song, and this is what He gave me. I titled it, "You Complete Me" partially in tribute to the horrifying lies presented in the movie "Jerry McGuire!" How many of you remember that romantic moment when Jerry (Tom Cruise) bursts into the meeting of the first wives' club and confesses his undying love for his lovely girlfriend, played by Renee Zellwegger. His crowning line, which melted the most embittered heart in the room, was "you complete me!" I'm sure every woman in the audience gave a quick elbow to their spouse and nodded, indicating those were the kinds of words to be said! Well, hang on there one minute! It may sound good! It certainly looked good, and I almost bought it, except for the fact it isn't true! Tom didn't complete Renee! We don't complete each other! That void is the God-shaped void, not the relationship void. You can't fix a vertical problem with a horizontal answer. In other words, when there is separation from God we need restoration with God, not a different human relationship. When it's a spiritual problem, we need a spiritual answer. The song goes like this,

"I was empty for so long,
Didn't know quite right from wrong
Believing the lies that I was told
Didn't matter what I tried, still emptiness inside

Cause I just couldn't see,

Chorus:

That You, You alone complete me
In You, I am made whole.
Bring Your healing waters to my soul
That I may truly know
That You alone, complete me.

Torn asunder, torn apart
Broken pieces of my heart
Not able to see the truth in You.
Every hurt and every pain, made less of me
Cause I just couldn't see,

Chorus:

Then in Your perfect kindness
Your Word revealed to me
Oh the value that I have in You
The way to be set free
From the lies, that seep into my life
That blind me from the truth
Of knowing, You're the Only One
With life abundantly.

Chorus:

And You, You alone, You complete me."

Beth Murray - 1999

Questions to discuss and ponder...

1. What are your thoughts on "transformational discipleship?" Does it resonate with your spirit? Has it been a part of your own experience?

2. Are you familiar with the process of "renewing your mind?" What does this look like on a daily basis?

3. Think of a time when you felt dismissed or patronized in regard to a serious issue/struggle in your life. How would you want to respond to someone going through a similar situation?

4. Discuss secularization and its impact on the church.

5. What experience have you had with secularization of the church—secular resources, training, ethics, etc. Are there areas where you agree or disagree?

6. Is there a difference between calling and purpose?

7. How have you viewed completion?

8. How can you speak hope and wholeness into the lives of broken and hurting people?

9. List five ideas for implementing transformational discipleship into your area of ministry involvement.

10. Assess your own spiritual journey. Where are you in the process of having Christ fill you with joy and satisfaction?

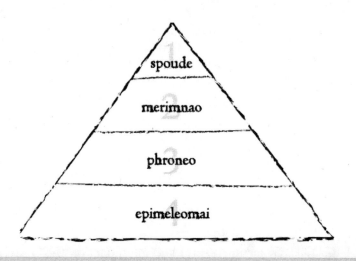

1. spoude
2. merimnao
3. phroneo
4. epimeleomai

I often use a metaphor of a river to symbolize the pain in our lives. When we discover the reality of our "river of pain," we find ourselves in the desert, usually tired and worn out from all the wandering we've been doing. We arrive at that river of pain and flop into a heap of depression and hopelessness. Why would God allow us to walk through this cruddy desert for so long, only to hit a seemingly huge obstacle like this river? Sometimes we just pull out a lawn chair, throw on our sunglasses and enjoy the desert landscape. This is usually cut short by the incessant heat and inadequate resources available to us there. If we look beyond the river, we catch a glimpse of beauty. There is a lushness and obvious life-restoring resources on the other side of the river, but how do we get there?! We can see the flowering meadows, the shade-giving trees and the sparkling waterfalls, and yet, it almost seems like a mirage. Every once in a while, we catch a whiff of the beautiful fragrances on the other side of the river, but nonetheless, they are on the other side of what seems an insurmountable challenge.

There is only one choice, one way to get to the Promised Land. We have to walk <u>through</u> the river of pain. Unfortunately, many people take one look at the ominous river and choose instead to become desert dwellers. They wander endlessly in the desert, never happy, always searching. They come to the edge of the river, but it looks too difficult. They want it to be easy and it isn't. So instead, they settle. They decide that living in the desert isn't so bad. They can survive the harsh elements and dangers. They've learned how to kill scorpions and snakes, and so, they settle into a nomadic emotional and spiritual existence. Oh, sometimes they come back to the river and look longingly towards the Promised Land, but they form speculations and arguments in their minds which convince them that it really is best to just stay put. It's easier that way. "Haven't I been through enough?" they ask.

The main question that plagues the desert dweller is "why?" Why'd it happen? Why me? Why now? Why...why...why? If you haven't learned this already, "why" isn't a very productive way to make progress! Part of our human nature is an incessant demand for answers. Maybe it's a direct result of the fall; the initial temptation, that we would "be like God." Hmmm, to know all the answers so we can know everything that's going on. "This happened because..." "That happened because..." I have all the answers! I have the keys to life and death, the knowledge of good and evil. I know WHY things happen! The problem is, we don't get to know all the answers! God in His omnipotence, is the One in control, with all the answers. The question that moves the desert dweller out of complacency is to ask "what now?"

Another group of people can see the Promised Land, and therefore don't consider desert living a viable option. They don't like the scorching heat and the creatures who inhabit the sandy territory. The thought of living outside of this horrible place appeals to them, and they come to the edge of the river. These are the toe-dippers. They tire of the desert—its heat and dust. They consider crossing the river on a fairly consistent basis. Their problem is they don't like pain! They hate the very thought of it, and long for a level of comfort they once knew. Why did things have to become so difficult? Isn't there a bridge? Or a helicopter? Or a boat they could use to get across the river? I mean really, the water smells foul, and it is rather scary looking in spots.

The toe-dippers come to the edge of the river, fueled with dissatisfaction about their life in the desert. Yet the moment they start to encounter the pain they pull out. Maybe the desert isn't so bad after all! At least they know what to expect there! They know it. They know the landscape of the desert and they are in control. The river of pain moves them into a place of powerlessness where they have no control. It's risky and they feel too vulnerable, so they pull back and retreat to the banks of the river. Once more they sit in the desert, pondering how they can get to the Promised Land without going through this frustrating river of pain. "God, why won't you just heal this pain? Take it away?? Dry up the river, or at least split it so I can walk safely through!" Sometimes God seems silent when you've got your toe in the river.

The big question for the toe-dippers is "how?!" "Isn't there another way? There's got to be a different way to make the pain go away." They spend more time trying to numb out the pain, avoid the pain, and bury the pain. For them the river really is

De-nile! (For those of you with a slower processor, that is a pun about denial!) Unfortunately the toe-dippers get so focused on trying to figure out an alternative means to crossing the river, that they never actually make it across the river. Some of them truly long to, but they get caught up in the weeds along the shoreline. Pain immobilizes them and blurs their vision from seeing the other side of the river, the Promised Land. The "how?!" question needs to become a "who." Who can help me get across the river?

A third group of people come to the edge of the river. They rarely look back to the desert as a viable option. They realize that life in the desert is severely limited and doesn't give them the resources and ability to have a good life. These are the ones who determine the only possibility is to walk through the pain, so they can live in freedom and healing in the Promised Land. If you think in recovery terms, the first group are the victims, enmeshed in their past and settling in a place of hopelessness. The second group are the survivors. They aren't going to be bound by their history, but they are merely living in survival mode. This third group consists of the overcomers or the victors. They don't deny their pasts or the damage done by them, but they choose to live above it. They want more! The thought of staying in the desert makes them nauseous, and they are compelled to "beat this thing."

The overcomer still hurts. As they walk into the river of pain they are overwhelmed. It's tempting to pull out and scramble back up on the shore! The pain hurts so much! Yet the air of hopefulness that has drawn them, catches their senses again. They must go on. Taking one step at a time they forge on through the river of pain. They can't look back, and they can barely look forward; the immediate need is to stand firm in the river. They take it step-by-step. Slowly, carefully, placing their foot on a rock that doesn't move. Then they stop and steady themselves. Sometimes the current tries to knock them down and sweep them away downstream. The journey is slow and the overcomer must take his time. He must only take as many steps at a time as he is able. The river didn't look this wide from the shore! And so it goes, taking a couple steps at a time, then standing still until he is able to take another step. The key for the overcomer, is that he doesn't run back out of the river, he pushes through the pain at whatever speed he is able. Soon he sees the Promised Land more clearly. He can see it, smell it, hear it, almost taste it! Yes, yes, there is hope! The river of pain can be crossed! He scrambles up the bank into the Promised Land and he is at rest.

The overcomer has questions, but they don't distract him from his goal to cross the river and get into the Promised Land. When the "Whys" and Whats" cloud his vision, he chooses to look above. He looks above to WHO can save him, his source. He looks above to who is able to grant him resilience and the ability to persevere. He leans upon God for strength and provision for the journey. He looks beyond the questions to the answer, who is Jesus Christ. His faith in God and a continued decision to trust Him, allowing him to carry on with forward movement. Illusions of control aside, the heart of the overcomer desires the freedom and healing that can only occur in the Promised Land.

Hebrews chapter four outlines God's promised rest for His people. Verse one says, "God's promise of entering his place of rest still stands, so we ought to tremble with fear that some of you might fail to get there." The Greek word for rest here is *katapauo*, which means "to settle down, to cause to desist, to give rest."[36] The Old Testament reference is Psalm 95:11, in which David recalls God's vow that the Israelites who hardened their hearts against Him "will never enter my place of rest." The Hebrew word for rest, is *menuwchah* (men-oo-khaw), which means "repose, peacefully, an abode: comfortable, ease, quiet, resting place, still."[37] Back in Hebrews 4 the writer says that even though God has prepared a place of rest for believers, "it did them no good because they didn't believe what God told them. For only we who believe can enter his place of rest." God's rest is there for us to enter, "if we don't harden our hearts" against Him. Verses nine through eleven read, "So there is a special rest still waiting for the people of God. For all who enter into God's rest will find rest from their labors, just as God rested after creating the world. Let us do our best to enter that place of rest."

I don't think it's coincidental that the last verse in that chapter tells us to "come boldly to the throne of our gracious God. There we will receive his mercy, and we will find grace to help us ***when we need it***" (as we need it). In the midst of the river of pain, while we're wandering in the desert or staring bleakly from the shore, we can come BOLDLY before the throne of God and receive grace, mercy and the help we need to cross through the river. God's desire for us is rest, to live in that place of rest in Him, in the Promised Land. We are meant to live peacefully, in a comfortable abode in our Lord. Have you ever had the pleasure of living, or staying, in a cozy, place where you felt entirely at ease? We recently moved out to a house in the country which is near a small lake. We hear birds constantly, are surrounded by trees, and enjoying the peacefulness of our little home. Whip me up a caramel latte with a wee shot of vanilla, and I am more than comfortable!

God wants us to make our home in Him. He is our resting place.

Reflect on your journey for a moment. Where are you? Are you in the midst of nomadic living, having accustomed yourself to the sun blazing down on you in the desert? Don't be content with the circumstances you are living in! There is hope! There is more to life than being a victim of your past. Your past does not get the privilege of defining your future! Press on! Are you dipping your toe in the river of pain, only to recoil and crawl back into your lawn chair? Hang in! Don't let the fear of the pain keep you from pressing through it! You've already survived your past, put it to rest! Walk on, my friend! Take a few deep breaths and do whatever it takes to press on and take one step at a time. Get the support from friends and professionals to walk through the river. Dig into God and believe Him to take you through the river. Wear Him and His Word as a life preserver around your waist. Take your time, but don't run back into the desert! Keep moving toward the Promised Land!!

Perhaps you are on your journey through the river of pain. Press on! Keep going! When you hear the taunting word "can't!", tell yourself, out loud, "I can, because I am." "Can't" is a shaming, defeating message, and it doesn't line up with a God who can! We often tell ourselves "I can't" when what we really mean is, "I don't want to do this!" Or perhaps we just need to admit that "This is really, really hard!" Take one step after another and catch hold of the healing and freedom you are receiving with each step. Feel it? Embrace it!! Hold desperately onto God and cry out to Him for whatever you need in the midst of your journey. Don't stop believing God. Don't harden your heart. Don't miss out on His resting place! God will enable you to get across the river of pain! "Do not be afraid, for I have ransomed you. I have called you by name; you are mine. When you go through deep waters and great trouble, I will be with you. When you go through rivers of difficulty, you will not drown! When you walk through the fire of oppression, you will not be burned up; the flames will not consume you (Isaiah 43:1-2)."

Perhaps you've even made it through the river and are resting in the Promised Land. Don't forget to go to the banks and cheer on those who are making their way through the river. They need the hope you can speak into their lives. Let them know that rest does exist, that there is freedom and healing and that you are waiting to embrace them when they arrive. Tell them about the rest and hope you've found! Scream it from the Promised Land so that even in the farthest reaches of the desert, they can hear your witness of the faithfulness of God.

This is why we need each other! This is why we need community, so that we can speak the faithfulness of God in our own lives, over and over again. A perfect opportunity for community at this level is to offer church-based support/recovery groups. Those who have made it through "the river" have a wonderful privilege available to them, to continue their journey by assisting in the operation of such programs. They can speak hope in a way that no one else can. Hebrews 3:13 tells us to "warn each other every day, as long as it is called 'today,' so that none of you will be deceived by sin and hardened against God. For if we are faithful to the end, trusting God just as firmly as when we first believed, *we will share in all that belongs to Christ.*"

One thing that I've seen harden peoples' hearts over and over again, keeping them from walking through their rivers of pain, is pride and wanting to maintain control of their lives. They don't want to trust God. After all, where was He when their trauma or offense occurred initially?? They haven't yet grasped the fact that control is merely an illusion. No matter how much we can "control," there are always uncontrollable factors that can interrupt our day, or even our lives. The pride seeps in with the battle of independence, "I can do this myself, my way." We don't want to submit to God's leading and what He is urging us to do. That's how our hearts become hardened, when we stop listening to the voice of God. When God is saying, "come" or "jump" and we are saying "NO!" When God, in His infinite, eternal perspective sees the next step we need to take for our own good, and therefore calls us to step out in faith, and we scream "NO!" We dig our heels in willfully, and lose our willingness. We become angry with God for "not hearing us," not "answering our prayers" and we harden our hearts. We are no longer soft and pliable, and we rebel against the very force that can save us, and bring us into the Promised Land.

You may wonder how this desert metaphor ties together with transformational discipleship and "care in the local church." My hope and prayer is you will see that every believer has the opportunity to live in the Promised Land, to enter the place of rest established by God for us. This is not about heaven and eternal rest, it is living in a place of rest during this present life time. I love Psalm 27 where it says, "I am still confident of this: I will see the goodness of the Lord in the land of the living. Wait for the Lord; be strong and take heart and wait for the Lord (vs. 13-14)." True fellowship and community takes place as intimacy levels grow and deepen. Sojourners who have passed through the river, have a deeper understanding of what it means to be real and partake of community. Facilitate this level of care within your congregation and you will notice a continuing movement toward authenticity and contentment.

God has a place of rest for us, and His desire is that we live in it presently! Our problem is that we don't like the fact that we have to cross through the river of pain to get there. Remember, the best property in the universe is waterfront Promised Land! "Though you have made me see troubles, many and bitter, you will restore my life again; from the depths of the earth you will again bring me up. You will increase my honor and comfort me once again (Ps. 71:20-21)."

Questions to discuss and ponder...

1. How can you most effectively work with someone who is a "desert dweller?"

2. What are the biggest differences between a "desert dweller" and a "toe dipper?"

3. Small groups play an integral part in seeing someone through the river of pain. List several ways a small group can facilitate sojourners on this journey.

4. Identify ways to minister to a "toe dipper" and encourage them to keep moving through the river of pain.

5. What makes a person an "overcomer?"

6. What kinds of care ministries could assist all three phases of walking through the river of pain?

7. Discuss the concept of rest and how it can be obtained during this lifetime.

8. How does the metaphor of the river of pain tie into the concept of transformational discipleship?

9. Where do you see yourself on this journey? If you are a desert dweller, what steps can you take to move forward? If you are a toe dipper, what would it take for you to forge ahead and become an overcomer? If you are an overcomer, how can you encourage those coming behind you?

10. Passage through the river of pain often occurs more than once. How can a person equip themselves and prepare for such a journey?

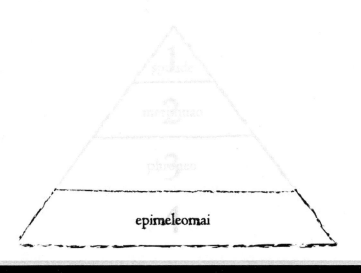

epimeleomai

As God has stirred this passionate call to write this book, I have discerned four levels of care described in the Bible. I will start from the bottom, or base level, and work my way up like a pyramid design. The fourth level is basic human care—*epimeleomai*—to provide care for. This is the Greek word for care that is used in the parable of the Good Samaritan. "He handed the innkeeper two pieces of silver and told him to **take care** of the man (Luke 10:35)." It implies a benevolent caring that occurs out of respect for human life and God. This parable comes on the heels of Jesus' response to the expert in religious law. The 'expert' asked Jesus, "Teacher, what must I do to receive eternal life?" Jesus asked the man for his interpretation of what the law says. When the man answered, "You must love the Lord your God with all your heart, all your soul, all your strength, and all your mind' and

'Love your neighbor as yourself." Jesus replied, "Right! Do this...and you will live! (10:25-28)."

Jesus concluded the parable of the Good Samaritan with a question, "Now which of these three would you say was a neighbor to the man who was attacked by bandits?' The man replied, "The one who showed him mercy." Then Jesus said, "Yes, now go and do the same (Luke 10:36-37)." To show mercy? To care? THAT was His answer and instruction regarding the greatest commandment?! You mean He didn't respond with, "Verily, verily, I say unto you, run evangelism programs, be seeker sensitive, host leadership seminars, and form ye a plethora of denominations!" Bear with me on this. As North American Christians, have we been faithfully fulfilling this most essential response to the "greatest commandment?" We don't do too badly with the "loving God with all your heart, soul, strength and mind," but the "neighbor as yourself" piece is a little much for most of us.

One contributing factor for this, is the epidemic proportions of Christians misled by Satan into believing they are not worthy of being loved, thus creating an entire generation of identity-less Christians. They wander the face of the earth, unable to love their neighbors, because they do not even love themselves. God assumes/presumes that we love ourselves, and creates us to have a sense of self-worth and identity in Him! He so completely designed us to know who we are, that the "neighbor as yourself" statement is written from God's perspective—that we do love ourselves because God made us lovable and acceptable, in the image of Christ—holders of the deposit of the Holy Spirit! God's perspective and design did not include the propensity for self-hatred that plagues and paralyzes the body of Christ! William Temple, an outstanding leader in modern Protestantism and champion of Christian social movements, writes these words regarding the view of self:

> *"Our dignity is that we are children of God, capable of communion with God, the object of the love of God— displayed to us on the cross—and destined for eternal fellowship with God. Our true value is not what we are worth in ourselves, but what we are worth to God, and that worth is bestowed upon us by the utterly gratuitous love of God."[38]*

In their book, "Love is Always Right," Josh McDowell and Norm Geisler challenge contemporary Christian thought regarding appropriate love of self. They point out that it is not a selfish act of love but a respecting of self, and a necessity for at least three Biblical reasons, "because we are made in God's image (Gen. 1:26)... because self-love is the basis for loving others...and because God loves us (I John 4:10)."[39] Proper love of self enables us to put aside shame, guilt, attitudes of judging, comparison, fear, inadequacy/inferiority and any other paralyzing emotional malady, in order to be fully available to God. If we do not care for ourselves properly, we cannot truly care for others. God has entrusted us with sole custody (or should I say, "soul" custody) of ourselves.

I love to use metaphors in my counselling (you are nodding profusely if you are a former client!) One that hits the point home for self-care is a person being like a gas station. They need to have their underground gas tanks filled up in order to pump out gas to those who are in "need of gas"/their care, e.g. children, spouse, friends, parents, etc. If the pumps are empty, there ain't no gas! Thus, when the people who need care from us pull up to our tanks, we have nothing to give. This not only affects those we are responsible to, it places us in a severe position of emotional and spiritual poverty. This can be remedied by tapping into the tremendous and abundant reserves of God's natural resources, to ensure that we remain "open for business!" The healthy individual also puts into his/her tank by engaging in healthy relationships, eating right, moderate exercise, adequate sleep, intellectual stimulation and being aware of one's own needs.

Whether we had effective or ineffective parents (or even the worst parents ever), we need to parent ourselves under the guidance of the Holy Spirit, and take personal responsibility for our own care. "It is normal and necessary for believers to nourish themselves to maturity mentally, physically, spiritually, and socially, and to protect themselves from harmful elements. This love regard for ourselves is the pattern for our love for others."[40] I love the gospel of Mark, for the patterns of Jesus' life that it reveals. Go ahead, read it right now! You'll see a healthy life rhythm of Jesus engaging in self-care and boundaries. He regularly prayed and had quiet times, then engaged in ministry and fellowship with the disciples. He went away by himself, practicing solitude, then engaged with the multitudes. He knew his limits (only because he was both fully divine AND fully human!) Jesus even said no! After being asked to continue healing and performing deliverance, Jesus said no, that he had to continue on to the next locale. "Wow! To not heal or deliver?? But those are good things! Ministry things!" Yes, you read that right, Jesus said "no" to ministry demands!

As a counsellor, I see client after client who has no sense of self-worth, practices self-hatred, neglects the care of self, and avoids personal responsibility. The end result, especially for a believer, is an ineffective Christian who honestly does not know the incredible power of Christ and the joy of a redeemed life! I'm not talking about salvation here, I'm talking about quality of life as a Christian, and effectiveness of Christian witness. I love "Winnie the Pooh," bless his compulsive-overeating little heart! Think for a moment, if you were to meet Eeyore and discover that he is a Christian. Would you be inclined to accept Christ, based on the witness you were seeing? Talk about your triumphant, victorious life (she wrote sarcastically!) "That's right, I found Jesus. But...oh bother, where'd I put him!" The same is true when we live defeated Christian lives, wherein we don't know and experience the truth of who we are in Christ. Jesus is the Light of the world—and as the saying goes, "the lights are on but nobody's home!"

Epimeleomai (say it five times really fast, like you mean it!) is closely linked to the word *melo*, a primary verb, which means "to be of interest to, i. e. to concern."[41] It signifies that something is an object of care. We see this word used in Luke 10:40, when Martha is "worrying over" her preparations, and the fact that her sister is domestically challenged! We see it again in I Cor. 7:21, 9:9 and I Timothy 3:5, where the continual message/interpretation is to worry over, and take care of. I Cor. 9:9 refers to caring for the ox—not muzzling him while he is working, and the fact that God is concerned about this dynamic of physical care. Verse 10 goes on to speak into issues of care and provision for God's workers.

The recurring theme of *epimeleomai* is reflective of provision, and to be concerned about basic needs. This bottom-line level of care provides a foundation for every other level of care, it is the "bedrock." Basic human needs are foundational to community and increasing levels of bonding and intimacy. When basic needs are met we continue to grow in relationship and meet ever increasing levels of need for love, acceptance, approval and completion. In the world of psychology, Abraham Maslow defined a "hierarchy of human need." He looked at the basics, all the way up to the emotional, mental and spiritual needs of the individual. As with what we see here, physical needs for food and shelter are foundational to enable further levels of care to be met. As it says in James 2:16, if we say "Well, good-bye and God bless you; stay warm and eat well" and do nothing to meet that person's physical needs, we miss the mark! In fact, our lack of action renders our faith useless and dead. The conviction continues in chapter 4 when James writes, "Remember, it is sin to know what you ought to do and then not do it."

I Timothy 3:5 outlines the elder's role and responsibility to take care of God's church, "but if a man does now know how to manage his own household, how will he take care (*melo*) of the church of God? (NASB)." The term *melo* includes an association of ideas. Similarly, Vine's Expository Dictionary of NT Words defines *epimeleomai* as involving forethought and provision (*epi*, indicating "the direction of the mind towards the object cared for.)"[42] This is the kind of care expressed in Mark 4:38, when the disciples and Jesus are caught in the storm and Jesus is sleeping in the boat. The disciples ask, "Teacher, do you not care that we are perishing?" Thankfully, Jesus was not as sarcastic as I am! I think I probably would have yawned, said, "um, no" and rolled over to go back to sleep!

In the parable of the lost sheep (John 10:13) we see that the hireling flees when he sees the wolf, as he "does not care about the sheep." In other words, he has no emotional attachment or sense of responsibility to the sheep. There is no personal investment on his part. He does not *melo* about the sheep. In modern day vernacular we might say, "he doesn't give a rip" about those wooly creatures entrusted to his care. It is the difference between being the owner of the sheep and being an employee, or should I say sheepboy/lamb wrangler/mutton manager.

The Old Testament Hebrew word *paqad* (pawkad) represents a similar level of care. It is a primary root word, which means to "visit by analogy to oversee, muster, charge, care for, miss, deposit, avenge, bestow, charge, commit, count, deliver to keep, enjoin, go see…, call to remembrance."[43] It is used numerous times throughout the Old Testament with an assorted number of variations in meaning. The underlying theme is a level of personally invested care from God to man, or one human being to another. One common example is the term, "God will surely take care of you," found in Genesis 50:24,25 and Exodus 13:19. One obvious implication of *paqad* is in regard to divine provision. Job 10:12 reads, "Your care has preserved my spirit (NKJV)." There is an element of trust involved in this level of care, where the person receiving care, trusts in the ability of the care-giver or fails to trust because of past experiences.

Paqad is the word used in the Old Testament when God refers to caring for the widows and orphans. In the King James version it is often translated as "visit." We are called to visit those who are in need. Visiting is a way to establish community and build a preliminary rapport with someone. It moves a person from acquaintance or stranger to someone that is invited in. If you have ever moved to a new area you know the warmth that comes from having a visit from someone who lives there. The same is true if you are sick or in the hospital.

Having a visit from another person simply because they took the time out of their day and made an effort to connect, does something for the soul. Visiting is an initial attempt to lay a foundation of care with another person. It is an invitation to take further steps toward building relationship.

When my boys and I moved to Arizona, we didn't know anybody. God had opened up an opportunity for me to work as a counsellor at a Christian inpatient eating disorder facility. The only catch is that it required a move from Alberta to Arizona! (When I prayed the prayer of Jabez, and that fateful line "enlarge my territory," I was thinking more along the lines of Edmonton, not Phoenix!) About the time we hit Flagstaff and the heat began baking us through the windshield, I lost it! I was thousands of miles away from home, driving through a desert filled with cacti and two boys in the throes of transition. I began to doubt my sanity as the loneliness set in, and I realized we had landed at another "new start." We had to stay in a hotel for a few days while we awaited our moving cannister to be delivered. Thankfully, we had a visitor quite soon after our arrival. Having someone greet me and speak my name, gave me enough of an anchoring to keep me from bolting and driving straight back to Canada! Hopefully you can see why this level of care is so foundational!

Questions to discuss and ponder...

1. What are your initial thoughts/responses to the phrase, "love yourself?"

2. Identify messages that have formed your view of self and the sources from which they came.

3. Why is proper love of self necessary for love and care of others?

4. What have your experiences been in regard to the foundational level of care discussed in this chapter?

5. Have you been in dire straights, experienced loss or been subjected to times or conditions of not having your basal needs met? If so, identify the emotions related to such an experience. If not, try to imagine and identify the feelings which would result.

6. In your area of ministry and responsibility, how can you establish this bedrock layer of care? Write down at least two ways you can express *epimeleomai* and practice it.

7. If you do not have this level of care established in your circle of influence, ask God to direct your thoughts toward basic care of others. Ask God to increase your propensity to care.

8. How can you care for the physical, basic needs of the poor and needy? Determine to follow through on at least one practical expression of care.

9. Discuss how heightening awareness of care issues in your small group or ministry area can affect bonding and intimacy within the group.

10. How can the issue of trust interfere with our ability to give or receive care?

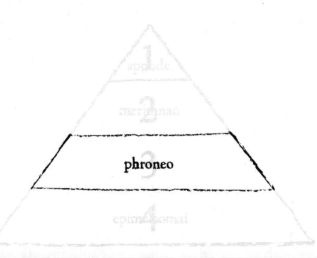

The third level of care is *phroneo* (fron-eh-o). This is a heightened level of concern or care that is personalized. Unlike the bare-bones, *epimeleomai* level, *phroneo* has a personal investment in the object or person being cared for. It is used in Phil. 4:10 where the Philippians are concerned about/for Paul, "But I rejoiced in the Lord greatly, that now at last you have revived your concern for me; indeed you were concerned before, but you lacked opportunity (NASB)." It includes a mental and emotional connection, in which the mind is engaged and exercised. According to Strong's "It means to entertain or have a sentiment or opinion; by implication to be (mentally) disposed (more or less earnestly in a certain direction); to interest oneself in (with concern or obedience)."[44] This is the kind of caring that creates healthy bonds in relationship. It breeds an "other" thought process, and a considerate and validating environment.

Vine's translates "be careful" in Phil. 4:10, to have a much wider range of meaning and "denotes to be minded, in whatever way."[45] A synonym for *phroneo*, is the English word affection. A similar word in the Greek is *thalpo*, which we see in Eph. 5:29 (as Christ cares for the church), and 1 Thess. 2:7 where Paul equates himself as being gentle with the Thessalonians, as "a nursing mother tenderly cares for her own children." *Thalpo/thallo*, means having great affection, "to warm, to brood, to foster; nourish or cherish."[46] This would involve a longing affection and nurturing spirit. For example, a dear friend being there for another dear friend in the midst of crisis.

Think about Paul's analogy for a moment of being like a nursing mother, tenderly caring for her baby. I can remember those days! There are few tugs of passionate care in a woman's heart, like those of cradling a sweet newborn by your heart (after they've been fed!) I would have given my life to protect that little bundle! It's the kind of thoughtful care that plagues your mind, even when you are away from the child. Every woman who's had a baby knows what can happen when a baby cries in the middle of a store, even if it's not your baby! Your ears have become tuned differently, your eyes scan more quickly and your physical senses are heightened to a whole new level of awareness. A new mother wakes up almost instantly when the breathing rhythm of her baby changes. This is the kind of care Paul is speaking of. A personal, deep caring, that grows out of increasing levels of awareness.

How does this relate to care in the body of Christ? It moves beyond the benevolent, generic care that we are to have for one another. It hooks into the human soul and breeds investment. The more invested a person is in relationship, the more motivated he or she is. There is often, but not always, mutual care at this level. As in the analogy of the nursing mother, the baby is not able to care for the mother, therefore the onus of care belongs to the parent. The child receives the care and benefits from it greatly, but its reciprocal care is primarily through the enjoyment of relationship and being able to love. Examples of this kind of care, would be ministering to children in a Sunday School class or club activity, mentoring relationships, pastoral care to those in need—whether it is a visit, providing financially or through gifts. The key being that there is a personal investment/attachment to the person, not just a food voucher or check in the mailbox.

Having been a single parent for almost twelve years now, I have needed this kind of care! Thankfully my immediate family has been amazing in this regard, and my parents have truly been there for me. Thanks Mum and Dad! Due to the geographical moves related to getting my education, however, we have been thousands of miles away from my family at times. I turned quickly to the body of Christ to assist me with issues of care. When I needed prayer, fellowship, a place to serve, I went first to the body of Christ. One on-going need that my boys had was for a "big brother," a man to be involved in their lives on a consistent basis. This was one of my greatest challenges (and biggest disappointments) in the church. The secular agencies have waiting lists so long that my boys could easily become "big brothers" before they ever got one! I turned to the church. I was thorough in looking for a godly man, who would commit to some regular interactions with my boys, one on one. The search was arduous and unfruitful for the most part. On several occasions, men agreed to the involvement, then quickly faded out of the picture due to their own changing schedules, and perhaps a lack of seeing immediate results/gratification.

Soon, I wondered if the broken promises were only doing more damage than the good of an occasional visit.

One day at seminary, a wonderful man named Jim, who was perhaps more boy than man, agreed to be a big brother to the boys. For a year and a half, Jim visited my guys on a weekly basis. He wrestled with them, played ball, made pizza, had belching contests, took them fishing, laughed with them, and talked to them. He became the first consistent male role model in their young lives. I don't know that Jim will ever know how deeply he impacted the lives of two young boys in Kentucky! Jim was Jesus with skin on. He showed *phroneo* and *thalpo/thallo* to my children. God bless you Jim for your investment into two children of God. After Kentucky, I again had difficulty in finding men to invest in the lives of my boys. Then a couple years later, a man named Rich took on the role of mentor and friend to my youngest son Scott. Rich faithfully picked Scott up on Wednesdays after school and took him out to play mini golf, watch movies, do errands and guy things, and of course, enjoy food together. Rich also modeled a healthy marital relationship for Scott, often bringing his wife along for supper or having Scott over to their home. Bless you Rich and Jan for investing in the care of my son!

In this scenario of care there is no mistaking the intentionality of the giver. The person receiving care feels an emotional response from the act of kindness or words of care. There is an emotional bonding that occurs as love puts on its hands and feet. An element of thoughtfulness is apparent, and the end result is that a person feels cared for, and knows they are cared for. It is an emotional, spiritual and mental experience of care. In his book "Connecting," Larry Crabb purports that healing of the deep wounds of the soul hinges on being connected with one another in increasingly intimate levels of care in community. "The power is found in connection, that profound meeting when the truest part of one soul meets the emptiest recesses in another and finds something there, when life passes from one to the other."[47]

I was just settling into bed when this example of *phroneo* came to my mind (yeah, I know, exciting life I lead!). When my boys and I were living in Kentucky and I was going to seminary, we lived in absolute poverty. The great thing was, everybody else did too! We all went to the seminary food bank, sat outside and watched tornados and storms for excitement (a whole other book!), played games and drank many coffees together. We made good friends fast, with not a lot of time for masks. We were all slugging away at one of the hardest things we'd ever faced, seminary! During this time while we were the poorest, we lived life the most fully. There was this great adventure we discovered not long after moving to Kentucky. Just outside of town, past the cock fighting rooster farm (yes, I speak the truth), there was a road that went right through the river! It was the best, free adventure for two young boys you could imagine! You approached the river at a decent speed, didn't slow down, and prayed that the waters would not wash your car away! (Don't worry Mum, we never did it after one of those torrential rains!) Water flew everywhere! Huge splashes went over top the car, as we cut a swath through that lazy river! It was such a rush, and the boys were thoroughly delighted by this thrill!

Another adventure we had, was learning to trust God's provision, and allow Him to work through His people and their hospitality. The last year we were in Kentucky, I realized we would never be closer to Florida than we were at that point.

I began to pray about Christmas and Florida. We were looking at spending Christmas by ourselves, away from family, and yes, in a foreign land. The next thing I knew, my good friend Susan, invited us to come down to Florida for Christmas. All we had to do was get there. Her Mom had a mobile home there, and we were welcome to come and go as we pleased. The only problem was, poverty! Nonetheless, I told the boys about our invitation and we put out the piggy bank and started to pray. We prayed and hoped that God wasn't a Southern Baptist, and that we'd be able to go to Disneyworld! (At that point, several Southern Baptist conventions were picketing Disney.)

Over the course of the next few weeks we continued to pray, and every spare penny went into our piggy bank. The boys even gave donations from their allowance. We prayed faithfully and my boys' eyes lit up whenever a dollar went into the bank. The next thing I knew, I was receiving unmarked envelopes in my seminary mailbox. They were filled with twenty dollar bills! The odd monetary gift was slipped through our mail slot at the apartment. Money was coming in from anonymous sources. The odd one had a note, but none of them were signed! (You know where this is going!) We ended up with enough money to pay our way down to Florida and back home, including all the traveling expenses, tickets to all the attractions (including Gatorland on Christmas Day! Gotta love those gator ribs and nuggets to commemorate the birth of our Lord and Savior! You did catch the part where I said I have two boys, right?!), food, and even a new battery for the car when it died in Georgia.

As Maxie Dunnam, the President of Asbury Seminary at that time would say, "God is good," and we would echo, "all the time!" Then he'd say "All the time," and we'd echo "God is good." Do you believe it? Do you believe that God IS good, all the time? He is! My boys tasted *phroneo* first hand, with the loving and sacrificial gifts of other seminary students and professors. *Phroneo* touches your heart and leaves you in a state of appreciation—wanting to give of your own self and resources to others. It is a reciprocal kind of care that breeds further acts of kindness and generosity.

Questions to discuss and ponder...

1. How does basic care move to a personalized level? What difference does this make to both the care giver and the one being cared for?

2. Think of an instance where you have received the *phroneo* level of care. How did that experience affect you spiritually, emotionally and mentally?

3. What does care look like in a ministry setting where there is intentionality on the part of the care giver?

4. List three ways a small group can foster this third level of care on a regular basis.

5. What obstacles do you foresee in trying to increase the degree of *phroneo* level care in your sphere of influence?

6. Reflecting on the two levels of care presented so far, how would you see them interacting (on a personal level and corporately?)

7. One of the struggles in cultivating a climate of care is the amount of energy required as opposed to the "visible" results. Success is often ambiguous and evasive in a microwave versus marinating culture. How can you instill the value of care when "facts and numbers" are the basis for assessing program effectiveness?

8. Think about a mentoring relationship wherein an adult is investing in the life of a child. Brainstorm five points of rationale that would support the development of such an adult/child program (remember the topic of cultural relevance.)

9. As a leader you need to be acquainted with the basic needs of those you work with. Ask God to open the eyes of your heart to the needs of those in your circle of care.

10. Discuss the concept of reciprocal care and how it impacts the landscape of the heart.

The second level of care comes from the word, *merimnao*. It refers to care within the body of Christ as in I Cor. 12:25, "so that all the members care for each other equally." In the Greek, it means to "be anxious about; care, take thought."[48] In II Cor. 11:28, Paul speaks of *merimnao* as a daily burden. Phil. 2:20 states that Timothy has *merimnao* for the Philippians, stating that he is rare - one who "genuinely cares for your welfare." In I Peter 5:7 we are to be in a position of continually "casting all your anxiety on Him, because He cares for you." John 12:6 uses the word in relation to Judas not caring about the poor. In Acts 18:17, *merimnao* refers to paying attention to a present situation.

Vine's refers to merimnao as "having a distracting care."[49] I've had those! A distracting care is when someone/thing continues to seep into your mind and demand attention, even while you are in the midst of other demands. As a single parent, I have had to leave a sick child with a friend, and go to work. Even in the most focused session, I still experience *merimnao*, that is, having a distracting care about how my son is doing. It has to do with taking thought about something or someone and have it be a cause for concern. Other occurrences of this word are used to represent a plea to not become overly concerned, distracted or worried. For example Matthew 6:25 & 28 Jesus talks about not worrying about our life, what we will eat, drink, etc. *Merimna* is thought to be connected with *merizo*, which means to be drawn in two different directions, distracted by a care, especially an anxious one.

In the Old Testament, there is a Hebrew word that casts similar light on this level of care. It is the word, *betach* (beh-takh), found in Jeremiah 49:31. It refers to "a place of refuge; safety, both the fact (security) and the feeling (trust). Assurance, boldly, without care, confidence, hope safe, secure, surely."[50] Is the church a place of refuge and safety? Do people find both security and trust in the church? Is this dynamic present within the body of Christ? I have seen it in action in spiritual friendships, small groups and even in some churches I have attended. The passage in Jeremiah refers to how easily a tribe can be wiped out when they have no *betach*—place of refuge and safety.

More than ever, believers need a *betach*. We're seeing signs of the end times all around us and if we're to make it through, we need each other! We need the prayer support, the accountability, the encouragement, the doctrinal truths, the worship, and the refreshing fellowship of the body of Christ! Isn't it interesting that current trends in church culture are movements away from connection and community?! Just when we most need each other, Satan is quietly luring and lulling people away from the fold, where he can pounce upon them and devour them in their isolated state. Beth Moore speaks to the urgency for transparency and unity as the body of Christ, "As the world grows more depraved, the church must grow more alert, more equipped, more sanctified, and more unified "so that you may become blameless and pure, children of God without fault in a crooked and depraved generation, in which you shine like stars in the universe as you hold out the word of life (Phil. 2:15-16)."[51] One star is nice but an entire nightscape filled with brilliant, sparkling stars is reason to ponder what you are seeing.

Betach is what I have in my small group. I have been in this small group for almost five years, although I was gone to Arizona for two of those years. This past year, my group graciously transitioned me back into their community. We have been doing a study on intercessory prayer and it has been fabulous, and so stretching! Beyond that, my small group is my refuge. Every time we meet together, we spend time in fellowship, study and prayer (and the odd time of mindless, silliness, just for fun!) In fact, we just sat through a service on "Recovering Your Belly Laugh" and we kept giggling and looking at each other, because we totally have the "belly laugh" down pat in our small group! Humour is so powerful in bonding, healing and forging friendships in, and through difficult times!

We go out for breakfast together and occasionally have lunches or other events as a group. I can say without hesitation that I absolutely love this group of women and couldn't function well without them. They have held me accountable on the writing of this book, often calling and asking me how

I'm doing. They aren't pressuring me to write, they are only holding me accountable to what God has called me to do, and they are also calling to assess whether they need to up their level of prayer coverage for me. I always welcome a phone call or visit from one of my small group members, they are a breath of fresh air. (Man, I hope they don't read this or I'll have to admit how much I really do love them! Kidding!!!!)

There is an investment in one another at this level of care, and the way we have grown to really know each other. We truly do bear one another's burdens. This past year has seen numerous changes for our group. There was the loss of one of our members due to unfortunate circumstances. One friend's husband left her and walked away after 22 years of marriage. One had financial stressors and difficult situations with some of her children. One walked through the death of a family member. I moved twice in that time period, and had to undergo sinus surgery. Through all of it, this small group was a refuge. Whether it was getting together to help move someone, pack boxes, escort someone to the lawyer's office, visit the hospital, drop off a gift, make a phone call, go out for breakfast/lunch/supper, go to a movie, or get together for study and prayer, we had a refuge. We have actively experienced *betach*. I must say that I like it and don't want to ever live without it!

Having toured the sites of the seven churches of Revelation, I was moved by the reading of the letters in each location. To actually place my feet in Ephesus, Smyrna, Pergamum, Thyatira, Sardis, Philadelphia and Laodicea, and read the applicable message to each church was life-changing! These were real messages, written to real churches, that existed in a specific space and time in history. Many of the dynamics described in the letters were evidenced by historical data and ruins. It was amazing! The words "suffering, hard work, perseverance, patient endurance, faith, and remain faithful" are cited throughout Revelation 2:1-3:22, with each message being ended with "anyone who is willing to hear should listen to the Spirit and understand what the Spirit is saying to the churches." To the churches in Ephesus and Sardis, the message was to return to what they first heard and learned from the gospel. Revelation 2:4-5 says "But I have this complaint against you. You don't love me *or each other* as you did at first! Look how far you have fallen from your first love (emphasis mine)!"

Each church addressed in Revelation had only a few verses spoken to them, and yet in the midst of a concise, timely message, two of the churches had a direct call back to that which they "heard and believed at first (Rev. 3:3)." God had complaints against these churches. The church in Ephesus lost their passion, the Pergamum church tolerated false teachers, Thyatira permitted false teaching, Sardis lost its vitality— becoming spiritually dead, and the church in Laodicea was lukewarm, being ambivalent and self-reliant. The church in Philadelphia was the only church not reprimanded in the messages in the Revelation. I can only imagine the list of complaints God would have against us, the church in North America, if a new Revelation was issued today!

An interesting note: Laodicea was several kilometres away from a mineral hot spring. Their water source was an aquaduct from the hot springs to the city. The people of Laodicea were well acquainted with lukewarm water! By the time the water traveled through the aquaduct it was neither hot nor cold, and had to be cooled or heated in order to be purposefully used. The Laodiceans were a wealthy people, well-versed in sports, education, philosophy, finance and the benefits of a bustling economy. They were known for medicinal eye ointments which were traded throughout the region. The message to the church in Laodicea urges them to "buy ointment for your eyes so you will be able to see...be diligent and turn from your indifference (3:19)!" Regaining passion for God and His people, rejecting false teachings/teachers, becoming vibrant and alive, shaking off complacency, and choosing to serve God fully and completely—these are the messages to the churches in Revelation. I think these messages are as appropriate today as they were in the time of John's Revelation!

You may wonder why I placed this level of care above the third level—*phroneo*. I did that because knowing ourselves and taking account of our own self-care is essential for care of the Body. If we don't love ourselves, we cannot love others rightly. In order for the body to function properly, each part needs to be healthy and effective. The finger that only wants to wipe the nose and never cleans or cares for itself, well...you figure it out! Also, to be truly effective in this level of care, the person must deal with the distracting dynamics of carrying concern for others. This involves the thought process and having to intentionally think about the well-being of another, particularly someone who is a brother or sister in Christ. This takes an act of the will, in which we choose to engage in caring for other people. When God places someone on our hearts, we have a choice. We can willingly care for them and respond to God's nudging, or we can willfully remove them from our heart and mind. I have occasionally called a friend and said, "Hey, God has placed you on my heart... and I was wondering if you could please get off!"

Have you ever been prayed for by someone who earnestly intercedes for you and cares about the outcome? What a humbling and bountiful blessing to have someone stand "in the gap" for you spiritually—to agonize in prayer over you and for you. We need to pray for one another like this. We need to break down the walls of independence that Satan has built around us and proclaim our need for one another. What God has designed is that we be interdependent with one another, and dependent on Him. It's fascinating to me that the polar opposites of dependence are both forms of mental illness. If you function in a place of utter independence, seared of conscience and need for human company, you end up in the vein of anti-social personality disorder. If you have no sense of self and live in ultimate dependence on others, you can end up with dependent personality disorder. The mid-point of balance and health is interdependence. This should be pretty straight forward to the Christian community, and yet many have bought into the illusion of control and fierce independence, looking to oneself rather than God.

Not surprisingly our culture facilitates such a belief. In the United States there is even a "Declaration of Independence." We see and hear a constant barrage of the purported necessity of independence. Themes like "looking out for number one," "get them before they get you" and "trust no one" perpetuate the movement away from community. Songs, movies, philosophies and education are all targeted toward the New Age phenomena of not needing anyone/anything outside of the self in order to be truly "enlightened." This was a tough point for many of my patients at the inpatient facility to grasp, especially if they were from a wealthy home. Their histories strongly supported the idea of independence, and it was often all they had ever known. Dependence was viewed as weakness, and external appearances were of utmost importance, even in

Christian homes. Interdependence was virtually unheard of, and independence was lauded as the only viable option.

Unfortunately, the end result of the independence philosophy has in many cases led to a focus on externals to the exclusion of self-definition. Thoughts, feelings and opinions are invalidated in lieu of what the societal norms dictate, and there is an overwhelming need to mask the true self. A few years ago a cartoon movie came out called "Mulan." Mulan is the story of a young woman in China who is trying desperately to please her family. In that time and culture the way for Mulan to bring honour to her family was through winning favour with the "matchmaker" and being assigned to a good man for marriage. After a terribly botched meeting with the "matchmaker," Mulan returns home to face the disappointment of her family. As she reflects on the devastating circumstances she finds herself in, she sings a song which contains the following line "when will my reflection show who I am inside?" Mulan was tired of having to play the part, and living with the shame of not being who she was supposed to be. Her own feelings, thoughts and opinions were invalidated and she found herself hiding behind a people-pleasing mask. Have you ever felt that way? If anyone knew the real you they wouldn't like you and you really wouldn't be acceptable to your parents, friends or family?

Sadly, some people have even been told that! (Just so you know, that's not normal and it's not right!!) What a shame to not be loved unconditionally for who you are! I'm so relieved to know we can find that unconditional love, *agape*, from God, our Father. If you have not found *agape* love from your parents, family or a friend, allow yourself to find it in God. The God who created you loves you unconditionally for who you are! He made you the way you are! One unfortunate circumstance I encounter on a regular basis is when someone has ineffective parents who have not been able to meet their needs for one reason or another. Unfortunately dysfunction breeds dysfunction, until somebody breaks the cycle and learns effective new skills and behaviours. At this point the person has a choice. It's a skill called "radical acceptance" and it is the choice to accept the reality of the situation one finds one's self in. It doesn't mean you like or condone the situation/circumstances, but you accept the fact that it is real. I've seen more people struggle along in misery, re-inventing their own suffering by refusing to accept reality. "I just can't accept that my alcoholic father doesn't meet my need for approval!" Well, the choices are: accept the fact that he doesn't, and get your needs met elsewhere—ultimately by God; or live in the continual disappointment of waiting for your father to do something he is incapable of, or unwilling to do.

Questions to discuss and ponder...

1. What are the primary differences between the third and second level of care?

2. Give some examples of your own experiences with *merimnao or betach* care.

3. Brainstorm several ways to implement this level of care into your sphere of influence—family, friends, small group, ministry area, work, etc.

4. What shifts are you starting to notice in regard to your view of the church and her responsibility to care for others? Is there any dissonance or imbalance between how you think, feel or act?

5. List one way that you can bring this second level of care into an authentic relationship between what you believe and how you act.

6. What is your biggest challenge to countering humanistic philosophy and knowing your worth and value in Christ?

7. As a leader, how does this chapter impact how you might work with individuals under your umbrella of responsibility who struggle with their self-identity?

8. Think about your own self-concept. What has helped you to discover who you really are and move towards personal integrity and authenticity? What has hindered that process?

9. Why is having *betach* increasingly important to the preservation of the church?

10. Vulnerability is essential for truly giving and receiving care. How does a small group/ministry area create a spirit of vulnerability that allows trust to develop and deepen?

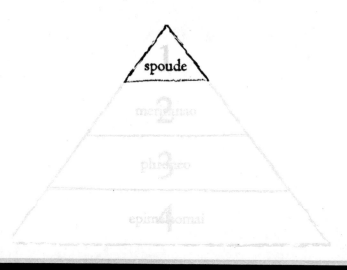

THE FIRST AND FOREMOST LEVEL
OF BIBLICAL CARE

The final level/top of the care pyramid is *spoude* (spoo-day), which means "to have earnest care, and diligence."[52] (These levels are not ordered in level of importance but how one opens the way for the next.) II Cor. 7:12b-13 says, "I wrote to you so that in the sight of God you could show how much you really do care for us. We have been encouraged by this." A couple words that stand out to me are "show," and "really." The implication is that *spoude* is obvious! It is evident, and it is a demonstrative expression of care that others can see. The word "really" brings to mind authenticity and integrity. In other words, you aren't faking this level of care! You really do care. It is genuine. In the movie "Shrek," Donkey wonders about the sincerity and trustworthiness of his large Ogre friend, Shrek, (probably because he spends a significant amount of time trying to get rid of Donkey initially!) As their friendship grows, they encounter a difficult situation and Donkey questions Shrek, asking him suspiciously, "Really?", to which Shrek responds gently, "Really, really." "You really care for me?" the question might be stated. *Spoude* replies, "Really, really!"

Further on in the passage, Paul is praising God for Titus and uses the word *spoude* to express enthusiasm. "I am thankful to God that he has given Titus the same enthusiasm (*spoude*) for you that I have." The crux of this form of care is that it is both deeply personal and love based. It has an emotional bond connected to a mental process and choosing. *Spoude* is intentional and implies deep commitment and motivation. It is a deep and expressive mode of care. You can't *spoude* someone without doing something about it! When was the last time you were enthusiastic—I mean, downright excited, charged up, having an adrenaline rush, about someone in your life that you care about? It's the kind of emotional response that comes from seeing a baby take his first step, leading your child to Christ or seeing God move powerfully in someone's life. It's exciting!

When I worked at the inpatient facility we had complete freedom to share the gospel message with patients. One thing I "had" to do, whenever I heard such news was to leap and scream joyfully, inviting others to join me in "the happy dance!" I would go from one office to another announcing that one of our sweet ladies had accepted Christ, and then burst into cheers of "Happy Dance!!!!!" Too bad I hadn't known the meaning of *spoude* back then, otherwise I could have said, "don't you *spoude*?" to the occasional person who thought my "happy dance" was unprofessional!

The primary difference between *merimna* and *spoude*, is that *merimna* conveys the thought of anxiety and concern, while *spoude* is about watchful interest and earnestness. The comparative adverb *spoudaioteros* signifies doing something more diligently and earnestly (found in Ph. 2:28, 2 Tim, 1:17, Titus 3:13, and Luke 7:4.)[53] Watchful interest and earnestness makes me think of the mother hen sitting on her eggs. She is constantly aware of their needs and takes caution to ensure they are kept warm and that she is gentle. Yet, beyond that, the hen waits in eager anticipation of what she knows will come. The first quiver of life, the hairline cracks in the shells, the tenacious writhing of the chicks to freedom from their oval nursery, followed by the shrill chirping of newborn chicks! Her watchful interest and earnestness has paid off!

This level of care reminds me of a song by Watermark that was sent to me by one of my former patients at the inpatient eating disorder facility. She was actually my first patient and took with her a piece of my heart when she discharged. I invested in her. I watched earnestly as her sweet spirit swam through the waters of deep trauma. She too spoke into my life with this song,

"Something brought you to my mind today, I thought about the funny ways you made me laugh, and yet I feel like it's okay to cry with you. Something 'bout just being with you, that when I leave, I feel like I've been with God. And that's the way it oughta be, yeah.

Chorus: 'Cause you've been more than a friend to me, you fight off my enemies, cause you've spoken the truth over my life. You'll never know what it means to me, just to know you've been on your knees for me, oh you have blessed my

life, more than you'll ever know. More than you'll ever know.

You had faith when I had none. You prayed God would bring me a brand new song, when I didn't think I could find the strength to sing. And all the while, I'm hoping that I'll do the kind of praying for you, that you've done for me. And that's the way, it oughta be yeah.

Chorus: You have carried me. You have taken upon a burden, that wasn't your own; may the blessing return to you a hundred fold. A hundred fold. "

Talk about a humbling and hope-filled encouragement to continue in the ministry of caring for others! Imagine if we touched each others' lives like this on a regular basis!

Spoude is a choice; it is a determination of the will, somewhat like *agape* love. I will diligently care for my children (even when they don't want me to now that they are teenagers! O.K., sometimes the enthusiasm quotient is missing but the decision to care is still there for the most part!) One of my favorite ways to show love to my rather large and continually growing 14 year old is to give him several consecutive taps on the bicep and reiterate the fact that my love language is physical touch! He sometimes offers to respond with "real" physical touch! In turn, he takes joy in knowing that he is taller than me. He often stands directly in front of me and acts like he can't see me! My new nickname is "Shorty" although I am 5'7"! His love language appears to be acts of service, although that could be developmental! He also receives love through time spent and verbal affirmations. My other love language is chocolate, and guess what? I'm multilingual—Belgian, Dutch, French, you name it. I can speak it and translate! It would appear I have the gifts of tongues AND interpretation!

Right about now you might be thinking, "okay, where are you going with this Beth?" Part of genuinely caring for someone is knowing them and allowing them to know you. Knowing is about intimacy. Being known is about intimacy. God created human beings to be known and to know intimacy through relationship with one another and with God. "Eeek, that sounds a lot like vulnerability and authenticity! I thought this book was about care! I didn't sign up for this!" If you haven't yet read Gary Chapman's "The Five Love Languages," read it! Discover how you most effectively receive love and learn how to effectively display love to those in your life. Take a moment and tap into your reflective self. Think back to a time when you most felt understood and cared for. Got it in your mind's eye? When was it? Where was the location/time? Who cared for you? Take a moment and write it out in the margin, in your journal, or on a sheet of paper.

What was it like to be known? To be cared for? Close your eyes and focus on how it felt emotionally. Are you smiling? Crying? Perhaps you can't remember such a time. Hold on dear one! God understands you and cares for you intimately. Psalm 139 says God searches us and knows us. He is intimately acquainted with all our ways and there is no place we can go where He is not present and available to us. I love how the New International Version puts it, "If I rise on the wings of the dawn, if I settle on the far side of the sea, even there your hand will guide me, your right hand hold me fast." Don't let your past define your future; it doesn't get that privilege! Just because you haven't experienced something before, doesn't mean you can't! Commit your future to God! Take down your walls and invite the Holy Spirit into those broken, hidden places to bring healing so that you can start to take appropriate risks that will allow you to be truly cared for.

In case you need some help with figuring out the emotions, there are seven basic painful emotions: sadness, anger, fear, pain, shame, guilt, loneliness, and one pleasant emotion, joy. The reason for the inequity is that we are very adept at identifying the pleasant emotions: happy, contented, peaceful, hopeful, excited, etc., all of which fit under the umbrella of joy. Come on, say it with me, "umbrella of joy." (You can even put your hands over your head like an umbrella!) I steer away from saying negative and positive emotions, because all emotions occur for a reason and though they may not be "pleasant" they are necessary. Emotions are the warning lights on our dashboard. They are meant to draw attention to what is going on "under the hood." If we ignore an emotion or render it negative and therefore avoid it, we may end up running out of gas or seizing the engine.

When our emotions are congruent with our thoughts and belief systems we find contentment. When what we feel lines up with what we think and believe, we find authenticity. We are able to be vulnerable and remove our masks. *Spoude* doesn't function within the realm of masks. Masks block contentment. They keep us floating in a sea of dissatisfaction, without an anchor. We become like the double-minded man in James 1 who is tossed by the wind like the surf of the sea, unstable in all his ways. It's hard to be stable when your internal plumb line is askew! A plumb line is a point of balance, the centre, to which things return. Remember those annoying, clacking, silver balls suspended in groups of four on many a desk in the eighties? If you pulled one of the silver balls back and released it, it would strike the other balls and set off a long, continual reaction of balls swinging back and forth. Eventually the balls would stop swinging and would return to their plumb line, the place of original balance.

So it is with us. We often encounter situations or people that pull us away from our original place of balance. If we have no plumb line, we don't return to it. If our thoughts, behaviors and feelings are incongruent, we will flail around and be directed from one external dictating force to another. In other words, if I don't have a plumb line to which I return in my beliefs, thoughts and feelings, I am constantly at the whim of external forces in my life. Who am I in THIS situation? With THAT person? Under THESE pressures? In THIS setting? This causes us to live as emotional schizophrenics, hearing the opposing messages which tear our souls and pull us in opposing directions. It is impossible to live authentically under these soul conditions. It's too risky to be vulnerable and allow people in. The walls go up and the masks stay on.

Questions to discuss and ponder...

1. Have you ever experienced *spoude?* Distinguish the differences of a care experience at this level.

2. As a ministry partner, how does (would) this foremost level of care affect you? When you are the recipient of *spoude* there is a brief glimpse into the heart of God—think of the emotional, mental and spiritual ramifications of regular intersections with this level of care.

3. How does determination of the will interface with the levels of care?

4. List several factors related to knowing and being known. (Consider benefits, risks, relationship components, spiritual issues, etc.)

5. Discuss the following statement, "being known is an intimacy AND integrity issue." Support your opinion.

6. From a Biblical standpoint, find at least three scriptures related to the issue of authenticity (that is, being genuine—being the same person, publicly and privately.)

7. What are the costs of mask-wearing? First, to the individual. Secondly, to friends and family.

8. How does the wearing of masks impact the body of Christ? How does it impact the spiritual health of the individual and their relationship with God?

9. Reflecting on the song by Watermark, is there someone in your life who has impacted you to this level? If so, take time to write them a note and make them aware of how they have affected your life (preferably handwritten as there is something deeply personal about receiving a handwritten letter/card in this electronic age.)

10. What can you do to move yourself one step closer to being able to give (and receive) this paramount level of care? (Be specific!)

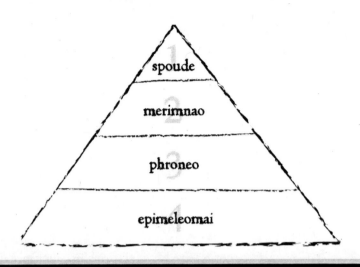

THE ROLE OF SUFFERING

There are many books written on the place of suffering in our lives, so I will not visit the topic in-depth. However, I think it is essential that we at least briefly consider the problem of suffering. Suffering has a way of blowing up masks, or creating them, depending on our coping skills and resources for support. When we suffer, we have choices. We can lash out and blame God, or we can lean hard into Him in the midst of suffering. Either way, we still must face the suffering before us. (Frankly, I'd rather go through it with God!) II Corinthians sheds light on suffering and comfort. Paul describes God as being the source of all comfort. In the New Living Translation, chapter 1, verses 3b through 7 reads like this,

"He is the source of every mercy and the God who comforts us.
He comforts us in all our troubles so that we can comfort others.

*When others are troubled, we will be able to give them the
same comfort God has given us. You can be sure that the more
we suffer for Christ, the more God will shower us with his
comfort through Christ. So when we are weighed down with
troubles, it is for your benefit and salvation! For when God
comforts us, it is so that we, in turn, can be an encouragement
to you. Then you can patiently endure the same things we suffer.
We are confident that as you share in suffering, you will also
share God's comfort."*

Suffering has a purpose. We may not like that it has
a purpose, but it does! It is for our own good, on many an
occasion, so that God can speak into our lives when He truly
has our attention. C.S. Lewis referred to pain as being God's
megaphone. I like to think I'm a pretty agreeable person and
fairly rational. I think I'm open to suggestions about change,
and I even seek God on what He desires of me. Yet, there is
often a two by four involved in God's finally getting through
to me in regard to the deep-seated pieces of who I am. Sigh! I
often think, "if He'd just have asked me nicely, I would have
changed that!" Unfortunately, God knows me better than I
know myself, and He knows what it really takes to bring about
heartfelt change in me. I wish it wasn't so difficult! I wish I
wasn't so willful and hard to convince! Can you relate?! I think
that's why the Israelites were always getting themselves into
trouble in the Old Testament. We just have such a mind of
our own! Our sin nature has powerful influence, although it is
sometimes very subtle, in wanting to call all the shots.

Remember the Old Testament story of the Israelites coming
through the Red Sea, having been freed from their slavery in
Egypt, and building the Golden Calf as soon as Moses is out of

their sight?! I used to think, "what's with those Israelites?! How could they see such powerful and obvious working of God in their lives and then turn and forget him so easily?" Well, I find that I do it myself, in more discreet ways. There's no Golden Calf on my lawn, but I quickly forget the faithfulness of God and panic when things go awry. I don't always go scampering directly back into the lap of God saying, "Praise you for all that I can learn through this trial!" Sometimes I scream, and cry, and flop into despair. Suffering is never easy.

When I was in my second year of college, I had some fairly major health problems. My immune system was crashing from the stress of the divorce, single parenting two little boys and going to college. One weekend, I went to my Mum and Dad's and as I went to leave, I noticed a linear rash on my back. I showed it to my Mum and she had never seen anything like it. It wasn't itchy but it didn't look very friendly, so I popped in to see my doctor on the way home. She took one look at it and handed me an entire box of pain killer samples and said, "You'll be needing these!" I had shingles! I thought that only old people and carpenters got shingles, but apparently not! The only prerequisite is having had chicken pox as a child, which I had done (quite well, if I recall!) The story I was told is that the chicken pox virus lies dormant in your system, unless you go through a period of significant stress, at which point it can "wake up" and become shingles.

Thankfully, we caught the shingles soon enough that I was able to go on a very strong and effective medication which cut the duration of the tormenting pain down from months and months to six weeks! I have never experienced such an agonizing, ongoing level of pain like that in my life (nor do I wish to repeat it!) It was like childbirth in sustained released form! It was almost impossible to keep going to school, let alone deal with all the other demands in my life. Not to mention the $200 medication that was needed. I remember a couple different people quoting Romans 8:28 to me, "All things work together for good, for those who love God and are called according to His purpose." Then they'd give me this hopeful, awkward smile, trying to convince me (and, I think themselves) that this was true! "Does this look like things are working together for good?" *I thought*! I wanted to scream!

One night in my frustration with the pat answers and the scripture quoting, I sat down with Romans 8:28 and had it out with God. God, in His infinite grace and patience with me, urged me to carry on and read verse 29. "So that those He predestined, would be conformed to the likeness of His Son..." That was all I needed to hear! Why didn't anyone every quote verse 29, alongside 28? All things work together for good, IF the good we are speaking of is that we become conformed to the likeness of Christ! Can I accept that?! YES! When we trust in God's character, to work eternal purposes in and through our lives, we will find that all things are worked together for good. It often isn't "good" as we would define good in our fallen nature, but good in light of God's eternal economy and becoming more and more like Christ. Yeah, I can work with that! Hebrews 2:10 tells us that "through the suffering of Jesus, God made him a perfect leader, one fit to bring them into their salvation." If Christ had to suffer to complete God's purposes, then why would I expect to avoid suffering?

Several verses throughout the New Testament normalize suffering. The Apostle Paul tells us to expect suffering, that it will happen. His ministry is packed with trials and suffering. He was shipwrecked, beaten, falsely accused, stoned, imprisoned, hungry and cold, etc. etc. Many Christians today would have pulled Paul aside and questioned him as to whether he was functioning within God's will! Oh "so very Job's comforters" we are! "What sin do you have in your life?" "Wow, you really get blasted when you step outside of the will of God don't you?" "Do you think God is trying to close the door, since this horrible thing has happened to you?" None, no, no! Suffering happens! Make a bumper sticker, people! Suffering isn't always about sin. In fact, if it is, we can see a logical sequence of consequence to a sinful action. God doesn't make a practice of slapping his children! If suffering is from the hand of God, it's for a redemptive, teaching purpose, and we know it! We may be resisting it with all our might, but we know in our hearts that God is speaking to us.

Why do we so often try to hang the burden of suffering around the neck of the wounded, so that we can injure them further?! Let me say it again, suffering happens. If we are moving in obedience to God's leading and a horrible thing happens to us or our family, who would be most likely to blame for that? God or Satan? Do not be naive, my friends. Satan does not want us to be effective followers of Christ, so if a door slams shut in a destructive way I would propose the finger prints you find on the doorknob will be those of Satan not God! And the appropriate response is to get up, push the door back open and continue in obedience. The God I serve doesn't lead, then slam the doors shut on you or your family, breaking bones or causing accidents! (That doesn't mean God doesn't close doors, but He doesn't do it in a way that is harmful and destructive!) Paul reports that Satan blocked his efforts and hindered him on more than one occasion (2 Cor. 12:7, 1 Thess. 2:18).

In the book of first Peter there are numerous references to

the topic of suffering. I Peter 3:13-5:10 has 14 occurrences of the word "suffer/suffering." Fourteen references in a handful of verses?! Perhaps suffering is more important for us to attend to than we think! Most Christians would rather hear about the blessings and abundance of being in relationship with God! But do we give God justice when we represent Him from the pulpit as God of abundant blessing, but deny the reality of suffering? The Greek word for "suffering/suffer" is *pascho* (pas-kho) and includes the forms of *patho* and *pentho*. It is a primary verb which means to "experience a sensation or impression (usually painful): feel, passion, suffer, vex." In regard to the references of the "sufferings of Christ" found in this passage, the Greek word is *pathema* (pathaymah); "something undergone, i.e. hardship or pain; subj. an emotion or influence: affection, affliction, motion, suffering."[54]

The sub-headings in these passage of scripture are "suffering for doing good," "living for God," "suffering for being a Christian," and "advice for elders and young men." Sounds like instructions to the church body, to me! Suffering appears to be normalized as a part of the Christian experience, concluded with "after you have suffered a little while, he will restore, support, and strengthen you, and he will place you on a firm foundation." It's noteworthy that two verses prior to this verse, is the warning, "Be careful! Watch out for attacks from the Devil, your great enemy. He prowls around like a roaring lion, looking for some victim to devour. Take a firm stand against him, and be strong in your faith." In light of the meaning of suffering, this is significant! Suffering is an emotional malady. It is an emotional experience, seated in the depths of the soul. So where does Satan, in his tremendous lack of scruples, hit us?! In the emotions, right in the depths of our soul. If Satan can knock us off course in the midst of our suffering he can devour us.

The implications are enormous! We, the church, must normalize struggle so that Christians don't isolate and pull away when they are most hurting! Our instructions are to act in the midst of our suffering—to be careful, to watch out, take a firm stand and be strong in our faith. These four responses to suffering, and guarding against further pain from Satan, are best done within the context of community. It is much easier to be careful, watch out, stand firmly and have our faith strengthened, in the midst of our brothers and sisters. If struggle is not normalized, there is far greater risk of shame-based reactions and a movement to hide and deny the issues. In this scenario, shame breeds secrecy, and secrecy blocks relationship, authenticity and vulnerability. Hypocrisy and a tragic focus on external appearances, become the mode of operation for the individual and often the family system, involved. The end result is a web of sin, spun into potential strongholds throughout the life and relationships of the person who is struggling.

When Paul addresses the Corinthians in his second letter, he reminds them that they are earthen beings. God has given us a precious treasure to be held in our weak and perishing bodies (yes, that's right, we are mortal and no amount of nipping, tucking, lifting, implanting, removing or snipping will change that!) The result is it removes the glory from us and puts it on God where it rightfully belongs. "Our glorious power is from God and is not our own" (vs. 7b). This description is a precursor to what I call the Mammogram verse, "I have been hard pressed on every side, crushed but not broken!" (If you are not laughing, please re-read that last sentence!) The NLT translates it, "We are pressed on every side by troubles, but we are not crushed and broken. We are perplexed, but we don't give up and quit. We are hunted down, but God never abandons us. We get knocked down, but we get up again and keep going. Through suffering, these bodies of ours constantly share in the death of Jesus so that the life of Jesus may also be seen in our bodies."

In my study tour through Greece and Turkey we visited Corinth and the Bema seat which was the place of judgment—the modern day equivalent of a court house. At the judgment seat someone had carved II Corinthians 4:17 into one of the stone tablets on the ground. "For our light and momentary troubles are achieving for us an eternal glory that far outweighs them all. So we fix our eyes not on what is seen, but on what is unseen. For what is seen is temporary, but what is unseen is eternal." Wow! For some of the Corinthians waiting in line before the Bema seat, the end result was potentially death, yet this potent reminder was carved into the stone. Our troubles/ sufferings on this earth, really are "light and momentary," in light of eternity and God's economy.

Romans 8:17-18 reiterates the message of II Corinthians 4:17, "...if we are to share his glory, we must also share his suffering. Yet what we suffer now is nothing compared to the glory he will give us later." It's too bad we are so intolerant of waiting and engaging in process! As Dutch Sheets says, "God is into marinating, not microwaving."[55] In my counselling practice I have discovered that most people want answers and change YESTERDAY! When I describe the "process" of healing, they are sometimes so discouraged they give up on the counselling and continue to pursue quick-fix and temporary solutions. Process directed by God's healing hand is often the hardest and most beneficial journey a person can ever engage in. I love the words of Romans 8:35-37, "Who shall separate us from the love of Christ? (*Notice it says **who**!*) Shall trouble or hardship or persecution or famine or nakedness or danger or sword?...No, in all these things we are more than conquerors (*not desert dwellers or toe-dippers, but overcomers*) through him who loved us."

The key to overcoming is "who." We overcome, we conquer these difficulties and problems, through Christ, because of His love for us. His love enables us to conquer. Verses 38-39 expound on the extent of this overcoming, "For I am convinced that neither death nor life, neither angels nor demons, neither the present nor the future, nor any powers, neither height nor depth, nor anything else in all creation, will be able to separate us from the love of God that is in Christ Jesus our Lord." Do you hear that, "NOTHING!" Suffering happens, AND nothing can separate us from the love of God. I do find it noteworthy that Paul doesn't mention our past. Neither the present nor the future can separate us from the love of God, but I have seen many clients who take their past and use it as a wedge between themselves and God. I don't believe God is blocked from loving us during that time but perhaps our holding the past between ourselves and God, blocks us from receiving His love.

As I stated earlier in this chapter it is essential to normalize struggle due to the resulting mis-perceptions in the church related to this topic. For example, if there is a spirit of pride in leadership, suffering is viewed as abnormal, something that shouldn't be happening. By viewing suffering as abnormal, we relegate something which is normal into a place where it then needs to be explained away. If suffering isn't normal, then what do we do with it when it happens? We tend to judge ourselves, or others, trying to find a "reason" for the suffering. This comes out of our eternal quest to be in power, to control our environment and manipulate our circumstances. "If I can find a reason then I can fix it," or at least blame it on someone/something else. James 5:11 reflects on the sufferings of Job, "We give great honor to those who endure under suffering. Job is an example of a man who endured patiently. From his experience we see how the Lord's plan finally ended in good *(Romans 8:28-29?!)*, for he is full of tenderness and mercy."

As a society, we have a low threshold for ambiguity—the grey areas in life—the questions to which there are more than one answer. Ambiguity makes us uncomfortable. It also accounts for about 75% of life! Many situations and questions have more than one "answer." Being unable to tolerate ambiguity is actually one of the leading causes of depression. We like to know the answer, and we certainly don't like having more than one answer. A low tolerance of ambiguity leads to a fear-based life, rather than a trust-based relationship with God and others. One of the major shifts of moving away from "the law" is encountering more ambiguity. Romans 14 addresses differing levels of faith maturity and how this shifts, "you may have the faith to believe that there is nothing wrong with what you are doing, but keep it between yourself and God...if you do anything you believe is not right, you are sinning" (22-23). In other words, our conscience in conjunction with the Holy Spirit becomes our guide, rather than the law.

Thinking back on the river of pain metaphor, refusing to tolerate ambiguity and accept the role of suffering, keeps the person in the desert. We can wander our lives away in the desert, having been freed from our captivity in Egypt but not knowing the freedom and grace God intends for us! Faith is ambiguous. Faith is the bridge between our own reasoning and an all-knowing, all-powerful God that we will never be able to comprehend. Faith is the bond that reassures us we are loved by God. Francois Fenelon, archbishop of Cambrian in 1695, comments on suffering and faith in his writings on Christian perfection. Fenelon writes,

> *"Peace of conscience, liberty of heart, the sweetness of abandoning ourselves in the hands of God, the joy of always seeing the light grow in our hearts, finally, freedom from the fears and insatiable desires of the times, multiply a hundredfold the happiness which the true children of God possess in the midst of their crosses, if they are faithful...thus we find his consolation in faith, and consequently hope in the midst of all sufferings."[56]*

Hope! Hope in the midst of ALL sufferings, is something we can only find in God!

Questions to discuss and ponder...

1. What is your initial response to the word "suffering?" Be honest! What is the first thought that comes to mind? What is your initial response emotionally?

2. How has suffering impacted your own spiritual life?

3. Have you been involved in a small group or ministry area during a trauma or crisis to one of its members? How did this impact the group/ministry area?

4. Why is it important to normalize suffering? How can this be done? (List four practical ways you can normalize suffering in your sphere of influence.)

5. Discuss the following statement, "To share in the sufferings of Christ is a privilege."

6. What role does trust play in relationship to suffering?

7. Ambiguity makes most of us uncomfortable—those grey areas in life. How does the fruit of the Spirit attend to ambiguity? Which portions of the fruit help **_you_** to face ambiguous situations?

8. Should is a bad word! It implies duty and obligation, and creates feelings of shame and false guilt. Either you are going to do something or you are not. Either you did something or you didn't. Track how many times you "should" on yourself in a day! Then purposefully attend to your use of the word should—work towards eliminating it from your vocabulary.

9. Review the quote from Francois Fenelon. What does hope look like in the midst of sufferings?

10. What role does the Holy Spirit play in our lives as we encounter suffering? Write down scripture verses that support your answer.

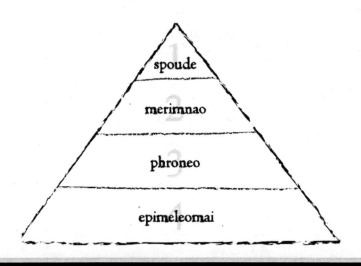

spoude

merimnao

phroneo

epimeleomai

So, Who Cares

O h my gosh! I can't believe you actually asked that question! How many more times must I say it?? WE must care! Why? Because it's our only option! The church, God's bride, is God's chosen means of expression and community on earth until the return of Christ. Are we the best looking bride? Do we really deserve the groom who is coming down the aisle?! Absolutely not! That's why I'm so eternally grateful for grace! Grace is the dynamic that turns us into the most radiant, breathtaking, acceptable and lovable bride. United with Christ for the ultimate and final completion of God's redemptive purposes. The ceremony is moving. The passion and love is palpable. There's not a dry eye in the place as the wedding of Jesus Christ with His bride—the church—takes place. "Do you Jesus, take the church on earth as your lawfully, wedded bride?"

Man, that's about the time I would burst in and say, "Um,

excuse me Jesus, but haven't you noticed how intensely flawed your bride is?! She's cheated on you! She's sooooo far from perfect! You can do better, so much better! Why, she doesn't even really know you! She doesn't even know herself! Her journal is filled with secret longings, mistakes and sins. Pathetic is one word that comes to mind! All the times You've given her second chances…all the grace and trust You've extended to her, and how has she repaid You? She's been so woefully distracted by all her baggage, Lord! She doesn't deserve a God like You! I object!"

Then Jesus would stretch out a silent, and reassuring finger on my mouth and say, "I know." His eyes brimming with tears and compassion, as He extends His hand to assist her. "In my eyes, she is beautiful—she is perfect."

I'm a big fan of Martina McBride. (Hold on you haters of country music, I said Martina, not every guttural, wailing country singer! Martina tackles some of the toughest issues with grace and care, speaking hope into darkness.) On her most recent self-titled CD, "Martina," there is a song entitled, "Wearing White." To me it represents how Christ will view us at the wedding to the church, His bride. It goes like this,

> *"Phones were ringing, tongues were wagging, hot gossip was flying all around town. She heard the talk, the lowdown was the shameless color of her wedding gown. It's white! I mean really, who's she trying to kid? Everybody knows the things she did! It just isn't right! Won't that be a sight, to see her wearing white.*
>
> *She was wild, a wayward child, to put it mildly, she made her life a mess. But she was young, the past is done. Now*

she's in love and putting on a new dress. It's white! And it's nobody's business what she wears. Anyway the truth is she don't care. Baby it's her life. She'll do what she likes and she likes wearing white.

He's all nerves when he sees her. As far as he's concerned, she's an angel...in white! He just can't believe that she is his. What a crazy miracle this is! Who she was he don't mind. Cause on their wedding night she'll be wearing white. She'll be wearing white. She'll be wearing white."

What a picture of grace and redemption! What really matters is how God views us.

Revelation 19:8 says the bride will have prepared herself for the wedding feast of the Lamb and she is "permitted to wear the finest white linen. (Fine linen represents the good deeds done by the people of God.)" We too, as the body of Christ, will be permitted to wear white at our wedding to Christ! Our purity comes from our relationship to Christ. We don't deserve to wear white, but we will get to because of what Christ has done for us, His bride. There is no greater love than what Christ has done and continues to do for us!

Christ didn't love the church because of her beauty, but rather how he could bring forth her beauty and loveliness. He saw what he could draw out of her. Christ sees the church for what He knows her to be, the beauty that lies within her, and what she is capable of. John Chrysostom paints this picture dramatically of Christ's love for the church, "For he who loves does not investigate character: love does not regard uncomeliness: on this account indeed is it called love because it oftentimes hath affection for an uncomely person. Thus also did Christ. He saw one who was uncomely…and He loved her, and He makes her young."[57] Uncomely is basically old English for ugly! Jesus chose to love us despite the fact that our sin has made us uncomely—ugly. He loves the church because He chooses to love the church, despite her flaws and ugliness. God's love makes the church beautiful and keeps "her young."

We cannot give up on the church! Satan would like nothing better than to see devout followers of Christ give up on the church and walk away. Disillusioned, frustrated and worn out, Christians are walking away from the institutional church in droves. I have talked to many Christian brothers and sisters all over North America and am hearing similar themes. Believers are fed up with the church and they are choosing to leave. Some are starting house churches, some are choosing to "commune with God in their own way," and some are just quitting. The Bible warns us not to forsake the fellowship of believers, the community of the saints. Hebrews 10:25 exhorts us, "Let us not give up meeting together, as some are in the habit of doing, but let us encourage one another–and all the more as you see the Day approaching." This verse is preceded by "let us consider how we may spur one another on toward love and good deeds." It's kinda hard to spur one another on if we don't spend time together! Firstly, I lose the right to speak into your life if we have no relationship, and secondly, the level of care would eventually cease to exist. The words "don't give up" imply that it will be difficult to stay in the habit of community. Being with a group of believers over the long term, has its moments! Notice the writer doesn't say, "Hang out together and if it gets too hard, just quit. All I expect is that you try." No, the writer says, "Don't!" "Don't give up!" This is all the more important as we are in the end times!

I believe that if we are to make it through the end times (that is the present day 'til Christ's return), we need each other desperately. We need to care for each other, to pray with and for each other, and we will need each other increasingly more as time continues. If the church weakens, becomes cultural irrelevant and ceases to care for its members, we will not be who we are supposed to be! No, it's not a matter of salvation, but as the Bride's fine linens are representative of her good works on the earth, we determine how we end. Will the church finish well? We can! The scriptures tell us the bride will be clothed in beauty for her Groom. Oh dear God, enable us to finish well!

Questions to discuss and ponder...

1. Sanctification is the process of being "set apart" and being made holy by God, and for God. It is both a crisis moment and an experiential process. I see it as a metaphor of a runner—positionally, Christ sets us into the starting blocks. We then experience a crisis moment when we fully surrender ourselves to Christ and are willing to have Him become our everything—that's the start of the race. Then we continue to be sanctified as we run the race that is set before us (Philippians 3:14). Where are you in this sanctification process?

2. What does sanctification have to do with the body of Christ?

3. List several ways that sanctification impacts the church (both lack of Christ's sanctifying work and the presence of progressive sanctification.)

4. As a ministry leader, how can you encourage those in your care and spur them on in their "race?" (Be specific! Write down five ways you can give practical, hands-on assistance.)

5. What does it mean to "finish well?" As a the local church? As the church universal?

6. What can you take from this book and implement into your ministry area? Recognizing a crisis in care in the church is a start but it is entirely meaningless unless it precipitates changes to how we do ministry.

7. Ask God to open the eyes of your heart and quicken your spirit. Ask the Lord God Almighty to give you revelation and enlightenment on how to increase hospitality, love and care to those He has entrusted to you.

8. Determine how you will attend to the spiritual well-being and protection of yourself and those in your circle of care. Be proactive in seeking the guidance, empowerment and equipping of the Holy Spirit in your life.

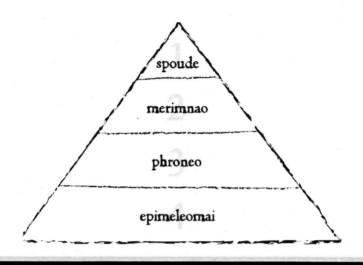

spoude

merimnao

phroneo

epimeleomai

Practical Ways to Establish Care in Your Church

- Low income car care clinics (mechanics in the church provide repairs for free and parts at cost.)
- Community kitchen programs/collective kitchen.
- Babysitting co-op.
- Handyman repairs for single parents, seniors and housebound persons.
- Lawn and yard maintenance services for those in need.
- Pastoral care by small group leaders for those under their umbrella of care.
- Think of ways to bless others—a small gift, an unsolicited act of service, a hug (provided the recipient is comfortable with physical touch), a visit, a verbal affirmation, etc.
- Visit someone who is in the psych ward, or prison—do an act of service for their family.

- Running errands for those who struggle with such tasks.
- Provide moving assistance to families and people with special needs.
- Shake hands with people you meet and give them your name, even if they are "undesirable."
- Transportation (give a ride to someone who needs to get to an appointment.)
- Visit someone who doesn't get out much, or have many visitors.
- Invite someone over for lunch after church.
- Pay for a camp scholarship for a child in need.
- If you don't have an active and growing benevolence fund, establish one! Fund raise as needed to facilitate compassion/care ministries.
- Drop off a basket of videos, popcorn and pop to a single parent family.
- Make eye contact with people who are on the outside. Don't ignore them! Say "hello" and reduce the amount of de-humanizing behaviour they encounter in a day— this makes forward movement in restoring dignity to another person.
- Deliver groceries to those who can't get out to shop.
- Offer to pay for babysitting so a young couple or single parent can attend a small group.
- Drop a coffee off to someone you've recently met at a church activity/event.
- Brainstorm ways to make your church community a caring body.
- Volunteer on a regular basis at a homeless shelter, food bank or other service for those in need (not to satiate your guilt but to embody Christ and extend love.)

- Offer free babysitting on Mother's and Father's Days for the single parents in your congregation—feed the kids and care for them while you provide a gourmet meal for the parents.
- Set up a clothing bank/exchange.
- Establish a food bank depot in your neighbourhood, or similar service ("We-can Food Co-op" bulk purchase of food for distribution at low prices.)
- Furniture resources/swap for families in need. People can donate their used furniture and household items through a network that matches the resources up with people need to set up a home.
- Scrapbooking or craft nights where free child care is provided, and benevolent assistance is available for those who can't afford to participate.
- Walk someone's dog for them.
- Deliver meals, pick up prescriptions and run errands for someone recovering from surgery (be especially mindful of single parents who have no family support to help out during such times.)
- Give beyond your tithe to help someone in need. Put a donation in an envelope and give it to someone anonymously.
- Build up a library of resources regarding parenting, stress, marriage, relationships, communication and child care.
- Welcome the new people in your community or church, with an invitation to your home for coffee and dessert.
- Have parties! Throw fun parties and extend your care to someone new each time. Play games, drink coffee, watch funny movies, talk, eat chocolate, and experience the joy of having fun together!

- Keep an "empty chair" policy (there's always room for a guest) in your small group and even in your home at meal times.
- Practice hospitality through phone calls, writing note cards, and stopping by to visit someone.
- Develop a network of support in your church. Compile a list of volunteers who are willing to care for others in some way. Get to know each other's gifts and abilities, and build a "helping network."
- Be an advocate for justice in your community.
- Be intentional in contacting people from your small group during the week, even if it's just a brief e-mail to say you are praying for them.
- Become a caring person! Do intentional acts of kindness.
- Invite a widowed person over for dinner and the evening.
- Listen for needs. When you can, respond to the need or pass it along to someone who is able to.
- Develop an emergency child care network for single parents and immigrant families who don't have extended family/support for times when their children are sick and they have to go to work.
- Do a "motives check;" "what is my motive for doing/saying this?" Is it love? If not, why not?
- As a small group, take on a service project for a local charity or helping agency—e.g. offer to paint a run-down office or center.
- Remember this saying, "but for the grace of God, go I."
- Establish and run recovery-based groups and ministries.

- Give from your excess, whether it is in the form of time, money, goods or services.
- Think outside the box!! Ask God for creativity on how to love others and provide care.
- "And what does the Lord require of you? To **act** <u>justly</u> and to **love** <u>mercy</u> and to walk humbly with your God (Micah 6:8)."

EPILOGUE

As I have been writing this book I have encountered a number of struggles and trials, a wonderful affirmation that I am on the right track! A few of my close friends have read the book and given me feedback. I've continued to dialogue with pastors and dedicated Christian leaders throughout Canada and the United States, and the messages are becoming more and more pronounced. The issue of care desperately needs to be addressed and changed in the Christian church! As I type this final word to you, I have experienced physical, emotional, spiritual and mental attack in various forms. I encountered a family crisis, am physically weakened by anemia, am on the waiting list for surgery, have been pummeled spiritually, emotionally and financially, and been hit by thoughts that were not within my normal experience. (I even had a sewer back-up, had to deal with the carpenter ant extermination, and even had a skunk

IN my house! And yes, he did leave his calling card!)

I admit I had a moment of regret for being obedient and writing this book. I knew that stepping out in faith, being obedient and potentially effective, made me a prime target for attack. "If I'm being obedient then things should just go along tickety-boo, right?" Not necessarily. God, the Creator of the Universe, does not owe me anything! It's not an economy of, if I do this for you, then You do this for me! I'll obey, if you bless me appropriately! Do I believe God will bless me for my obedience? Absolutely! Blessings however, come in many shapes and sizes, and some of them have an eternal redemption clause. Thankfully, God is gracious and we worked through my "little issue" and the writing continued!

I am so grateful to God for the privilege of being a vessel for Him to use in regard to this topic. I will open my mouth if God will fill it! I thank God for the privilege of sharing in the sufferings of Christ. May you take from this book all that God would desire to transcribe into your heart. May you be moved to love and care for others as God directs you. May you feel and know the love of God in your own life.

"For this reason I kneel before the Father, from whom his whole family in heaven and on earth derives its name. I pray that out of his glorious riches he may strengthen you with power through his Spirit in your inner being, so that Christ may dwell in your hearts through faith. And I pray that you, being rooted and established in love, may have power, together with all the saints, to grasp how wide and long and high and deep is the love of Christ, and to know this love that surpasses knowledge—that you may be filled to the measure of all the fullness of God. Now to him who is able to do immeasurably more than all we ask or imagine, according to his power that is

at work within us, to him be glory in the church and in Christ
Jesus throughout all generations, for ever and ever! Amen."
Eph. 3:14-21.

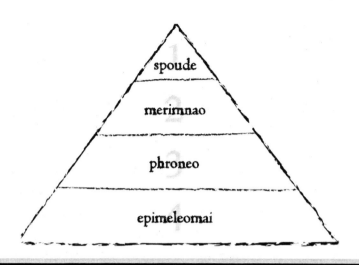

spoude

merimnao

phroneo

epimeleomai

POST-EPILOGUE

You might be wondering if this book will ever end! The answer is yes! It is now the end of December and my faith has been tested again. Trials have increased and my hands were ripped raw by having to grab hold of trust in a much deeper way. For the months following the writing of this book, I experienced increasing health problems which culminated in major surgery on November 5/2004. Since that time, I have been experiencing the process of recovery and healing. Shortly after returning home I was diagnosed with a deep tissue infection and went on heavy doses of two front-line antibiotics. Three and a half weeks of medication followed and I began to feel more and more unwell. The surgeon was seeing me weekly and ordered an ultrasound to determine any further cause to my discomfort. The results revealed an abscess. After five weeks of recovery I was re-admitted to hospital and placed on intravenous antibiotics. Blood tests were done and high doses of antibiotics were administered. Interns came in and groped me, "the abcess in bed 35b."

This was definitely disrupting my life! Over the last couple of months, I had put together a proposal for our church to develop a care department and strengthen the pastoral care component of our ministry. The proposal was moving along well and I was also moving towards being accredited as a member of the clergy, and shifting from a contract position to a permanent, full-time position. My accreditation interview was slated for Wednesday, December 15. I was re-admitted on the 10th! I wrestled with God and I struggled with the re-admittance to the hospital. I KNOW and BELIEVE that God heals! I believe fully in the divine healing power of God! Yet, there I sat in a hospital bed with an IV pole as my best friend. The surgeon explained that I would be in the hospital for another 7-10 days of antibiotic therapy followed by surgery to remove the abscess. He also explained that he would in all likelihood have to re-open the entire incision and I would be looking at an additional six-eight weeks of recovery and being off work. UGH! NO!!!

That day I cried out to God relentlessly. How could I possibly endure this? How could I manage another major surgery and all the demands that go with it? Who would help care for me this time—everyone was taxed to the breaking point. Who would help with my kids? How would I ever be able to get back on top of my bills? I'd be in the hospital for Christmas!

God gave me two pieces of scripture that day, Isaiah 8:11-14a, "The Lord has said to me in the strongest terms: Do not think like everyone else does. Do not be afraid that some plan conceived behind closed doors will be the end of you. Do not fear anything except the Lord Almighty. He alone is the Holy One. If you fear him, you need fear nothing else. He will keep you safe." I underlined this passage and dated it in my Bible, "December 12/04." I committed it to memory and ran it over and over in my head. Then He gave me Psalm 112:7-8, "They do not fear bad news; they confidently trust the Lord to care for them. They are confident and fearless and can face their foes triumphantly."

This became the second part of my "trust mantra." I reeled emotionally yet I clung to the truth of these two passages. I had a choice to make—to trust, or not to trust. Was I willing to submit myself to WHATEVER God determined to do in this situation? Did I trust that His purposes were bigger and more important than mine, even if they hurt? Could I really speak the words of Philippians 1:29, "For you have been given not only the privilege of trusting in Christ but also the privilege of suffering for him." Privilege?! For real?! Then it struck me to the core of my being and I was deeply humbled. "Are you willing?" The phrase echoed in my head, over and over again. "Are you willing to trust Me and obey Me?" One of the hardest moments of my life was when I uttered a "yes!" to this question.

The mental and emotional anguish continued to hit in small waves but quickly subsided as I recited my "trust mantra." The next day consisted of no food and water, and an attempt to drain the abscess by guided ultrasound. The attempt was unsuccessful as the fluid was too thick. The ultrasound physician was able to get a tiny sampling of fluid to send to the lab to assess the nature of the infection more specifically. I was allowed to eat supper and was placed back on fasting to prepare for probable surgery the next day. In the morning, an intern came in and asked me when my surgery was. I stated that I wasn't sure that I was having surgery! A couple of hours later my surgeon came in with a relieved and somewhat puzzled look, explaining that the abscess was actually a hematoma (essentially a pocket of clotted blood which will absorb into my system) and the pathology reports showed that there was absolutely no infection! I was discharged and allowed to go home!

Coincidence, or GOD-incidence?! The surgeon couldn't explain it, but I could. Many, many people were holding me up in prayer and asking God for His healing, miraculous touch upon my body. I went into the hospital with an infection-ridden body and an abscess; I came home four days later with a blood bruise and overall good health! Praise God for His unfailing love and faithfulness! Praise God that I was able to trust Him confidently and thus grow in my faith. Praise God, that by His strength and provision, I was able to surrender myself to His care and remain willing.

The next day I attended my accreditation interview and oral examination. I did especially well on the questions related to healing! I am now an accredited member of the Christian and Missionary Alliance Church of Canada. Last week I received news that I will begin full-time, permanent employment with Beulah Alliance Church on January 1, 2005! The accreditation that was once an impossibility due to being a divorced woman has been championed by my God, and the year long process of waiting for the door to open to full-time ministry has been opened. I WILL confidently trust the Lord to care for me.

May this be a source of encouragement and challenge to you as you call upon God and look to Him as your provision. He IS faithful!! Are YOU willing?

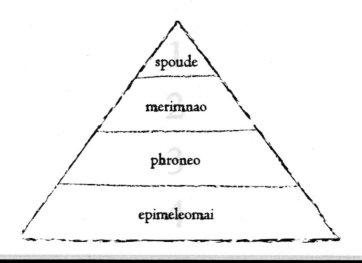

spoude

merimnao

phroneo

epimeleomai

Endnotes

1. James Strong, *The New Strong's Exhaustive Concordance of the Bible* (Nashville, TN: Thomas Nelson Publishers, 1990), ref. no. 34.

2. Larry Crabb, *Soul Talk* (Nashville, TN: Integrity Publishers, 2003), 123.

3. Christine D. Pohl, *Making Room; Recovering Hospitality as a Christian Tradition* (Grand Rapids, MI: William B. Eerdmans Publishing Company, 1999), 5.

4. Ibid., 4.

5. Ibid., 5.

6. Ibid., 6.

7. Ibid., 4.

8. Thomas C. Oden, *Life in the Spirit; Systematic Theology: Volume Three* (San Francisco: Harper Collins, 1992), 301.

9. Ibid., 301.

10. Larry Crabb, *Connecting* (Dallas, TX: Word Publishing, 1997), 83.

11. C.S. Lewis, *The Complete C.S. Lewis Signature Classics* (San Francisco: Harper Collins, 2002), 407.

12. Thomas C. Oden, *Life in the Spirit; Systematic Theology: Volume Three*, 272-73.

13. Ibid., 319.

14. Ibid., 318.

15. Ibid., 319.

16. Strong, *The New Strong's Exhaustive Concordance of the Bible*, ref. no. 5503.

17. Thomas C. Oden, *Life in the Spirit; Systematic Theology: Volume Three*, 270.

18. Ibid., 334.

19. Ibid., 335.

20. Thomas Merton, *New Seeds of Contemplation* (New York: New Directions Paperbook, 1972), 71.

21. Ibid., 72.

22. Hugh T. Kerr (Editor), *Readings in Christian Thought; second edition* (Nashville, TN: Abingdon Press, 1990), 258.

23. Christine D. Pohl, *Making Room; Recovering Hospitality as a Christian Tradition*, 53.

24. Larry Crabb, *Soul Talk*, 98.

25. Randy Alcorn, *Grace and Truth* (Sisters, OR: Multnomah Publishers, 2003), 87.

26. Paul Tournier, *The Whole Person in a Broken World* (New York: Harper & Row, 1964), 159.

27. Ibid., 70.

28. Strong, *The New Strong's Exhaustive Concordance of the Bible*, ref. no. 1531.

29. Blue Letter Bible. "Dictionary and Word Search for

'sumpnigo (Strong's 4846) '" . Blue Letter Bible. 1996-2002. 21 Feb 2005.

30. Blue Letter Bible. "Dictionary and Word Search for 'akarpos (Strong's 175) '" . Blue Letter Bible. 1996-2002. 21 Feb 2005.

31. Blue Letter Bible. "Dictionary and Word Search for 'ploutos (Strong's 4149) '" . Blue Letter Bible. 1996-2002. 21 Feb 2005.

32. Beth Moore, *When Godly People do Ungodly Things* (Nashville, TN: Broadman & Holman Publishers, 2002), 246.

33. Ibid., 247.

34. Dutch Sheets, *Intercessory Prayer* (Ventura, CA: Regal Books, 1996), 28.

35. Beth Moore, *When Godly People do Ungodly Things*, 183.

36. Blue Letter Bible. "Dictionary and Word Search for 'ploutos (Strong's 4149) '" . Blue Letter Bible. 1996-2002. 21 Feb 2005.

37. Blue Letter Bible. "Dictionary and Word Search for 'manuwchah (Strong's 04496) '" . Blue Letter Bible. 1996-2002. 21 Feb 2005.

38. Richard J. Foster and James Bryan Smith (editors), *Devotional Classics* (San Francisco: Harper Collins, 1990), 254.

39. Josh McDowell & Norm Geisler, *Love is Always Right* (Dallas, TX: Word Publishing, 1996), 104.

40. Ibid., 105.

41. Strong, *The New Strong's Exhaustive Concordance of the Bible*, ref. no. 3199.

42. W.E. Vine and Merrill F. Unger, *Vine's Complete Expository Dictionary of Old and New Testament Words* (Nashville, TN: Nelson Reference, 1996), ref. no. 1959.

43. Strong, *The New Strong's Exhaustive Concordance of the Bible*, ref. no. 6485.

44. Ibid., ref. no. 5426.

45. W.E. Vine and Merrill F. Unger, *Vine's Complete Expository Dictionary of Old and New Testament Words*, ref. no. 5426.

46. Strong, *The New Strong's Exhaustive Concordance of the Bible*, ref. no. 2282.

47. Larry Crabb, *Connecting*, 31.

48. Strong, *The New Strong's Exhaustive Concordance of the Bible*, 3309.

49. W. E. Vine and Merrill F. Unger, *Vine's Complete Expository Dictionary of Old and New Testament Words*, ref. no. 3309.

50. Strong, *The New Strong's Exhaustive Concordance of the Bible*, ref. no. 983.

51. Beth Moore, *When Godly People do Ungodly Things*, 133.

52. Strong, *The New Strong's Exhaustive Concordance of the Bible*, ref. no. 4710.

53. Ibid., ref. no. 4707.

54. Ibid., ref. no. 3958.

55. Dutch Sheets, *Intercessory Prayer*, 38.

56. Richard J. Foster and James Bryan Smith, *Devotional Classics*, 46-47.

57. Thomas C. Oden, *Life in the Spirit; Systematic Theology: Volume Three*, 318.

ISBN 1-41205388-9